FAST AND FURIOUS

FAST AND FURIOUS

BARACK OBAMA'S BLOODIEST SCANDAL AND ITS SHAMELESS COVER-UP

KATIE PAVLICH

Since 1947
REGNERY
PUBLISHING, INC.
An Eagle Publishing Company • Washington, DC

Library of Congress Cataloging-in-Publication Data

Pavlich, Katie.
  Fast and furious / by Katie Pavlich.
    p. cm.
  ISBN 978-1-59698-321-2
  1. United States. Bureau of Alcohol, Tobacco, Firearms, and
Explosives. 2. Illegal arms transfers--Mexican-American Border Region.
I. Title.
  HV8144.B87P38 2012
  363.25'9336--dc23
                          2012005550

Published in the United States by
Regnery Publishing, Inc.
One Massachusetts Avenue NW
Washington, DC 20001
www.Regnery.com

Manufactured in the United States of America
10 9 8 7 6 5 4 3 2 1

Books are available in quantity for promotional or premium use. Write to Director of Special Sales, Regnery Publishing, Inc., One Massachusetts Avenue NW, Washington, DC 20001, for information on discounts and terms or call (202) 216-0600.

Distributed to the trade by
Perseus Distribution
387 Park Avenue South
New York, NY 10016

To those who have the courage to stand for truth.
To my parents for teaching me how to take on a challenge.

CONTENTS

INTRODUCTION

by ATF Special Agent Jay Dobyns

When it became known that the weapons found at the ambush murder scene of United States Border Patrol Agent Brian Terry had willingly been allowed to pass through the hands of my agency during Operation Fast and Furious, all of my peers were in shock and disbelief. I wasn't.

In the years leading up to the tragedy in Peck Canyon, Arizona— just a few miles down the road from where I grew up—I had become a first-hand witness to the decay of the federal law enforcement agency I love and had dedicated my entire adult life to serving: the United

States Department of Justice's Bureau of Alcohol, Tobacco, Firearms and Explosives.

When I became an ATF agent twenty-five years ago, I was hired on to an agency administered by hard men with hard-earned law enforcement experience. Many ATF managers had been trained in the responsibilities of policing in prior careers as local patrol officers and detectives.

ATF agents brought with them a real-life understanding of what it meant to be a cop—how to run investigations and handle informants, all the elements of cops and robbers. As they moved up the ranks, they carried themselves with enormous self-esteem and confidence, having cut their teeth as real policemen well before becoming federal agents. They were full of pride that they had earned their stripes by getting "in the weeds" as investigators. They were intelligent and experienced lawmen who eventually rose to positions of influence in ATF.

As ATF managers, they were fearless men who knew what it felt like to have a criminal point a gun in their face. They had chased drug dealers down alleys, wrestling them to the ground. They had left wives and babies behind at home, while diligently spending endless days and nights on stakeouts with nothing more to show for it than a backseat full of fast food wrappers. They had kicked in doors as point men on search warrants, unsure of what waited for them on the other side. They grew beards and bought guns and bombs undercover from society's most dangerous felons. They were policemen and law enforcement officers first and foremost, executive bureaucrats a distant second.

These are the people who once directed ATF. Were they perfect? Of course not. Did they make mistakes? You bet they did. But they called the shots and were not afraid to make decisions. They didn't feel they had to run to a government attorney to tell them what was, or was not, the right thing to do. They didn't conduct secret, hidden, surreptitious programs, because they didn't have to. Our mission was clear and pure and they demanded we hold to it.

In the rookie agents they interviewed and hired, the "old dogs" looked for and expected a standard of performance and courage equal to their own. There was a sense of mentorship. They cared about their people. They were demanding of them, but with a sense of compassion for new agents trying to learn and make their way.

ATF agents were street cops with gold badges. We played hard but worked harder. We would join forces with our federal, state, and local partners and never care about who claimed the "stats." We were just churnin' and burnin' to put the bad guys behind bars.

It's not entirely clear when or why things changed, but it is perfectly clear that they did; every veteran ATF agent knows it happened. Some people claim it began after ATF's raid of the Branch Davidian compound in Waco, Texas, in 1993. Some say it was when government was realigned and ATF was moved from the Treasury Department to the Department of Justice in 2003. Either way, the hardness of the ATF began to dissolve and was replaced by a more intellectual, and deceptive, view of how we investigate crime.

The old bosses who stuffed worn-out six-shot Smith and Wesson revolvers in the back waistband of their Sears and Roebuck suits were being replaced by bosses with well-polished Sig Sauer's and slick monogrammed shirts with cuff-links, who were very careful not to let any gun oil get on their Armani jackets. Bosses who wore jeans and cowboy boots to work were being pushed out by newcomers with Dockers and tasseled loafers.

The mentality of the agency shifted from down-and-dirty everyday police work pursuing criminals to a newer, cleaner version where statistics and appearance reigned supreme. While we once chased after felons with guns and scraped our knees doing it, we were now encouraged to sit behind computer screens and electronically investigate syndicates.

The old bosses who had spent a dozen years on the street perfecting the craft of being ATF agents were supplanted by two- and three-year "wunderkinds." Street knowledge was no longer important; the agents who got promoted were the ones who wore suits and ties rather than street work clothes. ATF agents were routinely promoted into management without any experience of slapping handcuffs on a suspect, writing an affidavit for a search warrant, or testifying in a criminal court. New administrators were chosen not on the basis of experience and performance in the field, but on test scores, and many chose to sit and study for tests and get promoted rather than do the traditional down-and-dirty work of an old-style ATF agent.

You get a reputation as a cop. Failing on the street is devastating. It creates danger for the officer and risk to his partners. When it became impossible for some ATF agents to "cut it" on the street, they took the "early up" option, worked on getting good test scores, and were promoted. Without real street experience, many became the equivalent of third grade teachers with guns—they took attendance and graded reports with no real understanding what an agent does and how he or she does it.

Some of those chosen began to climb the government's corporate ladder. They nodded approval to the bad ideas of those above them for fear of being knocked off their personal ascent. They took care of each other and defended or ignored failed leadership because, after all, "I could be next."

Ultimately some of the "yes men" with empty character and empty experience landed in positions of significant influence. They told agents how to do their jobs—even if they were often failed street agents themselves. As supervisors, they looked down on field agents and were unwilling to listen to questions, take advice, or hear complaints from anyone ranked below them. The common response from executives to questions or complaints: "You don't understand the big picture. Now that I am an executive and you are a mere street 'hump' I am right and you are wrong." The attitude was, "My title is more important than yours, therefore I know more that you."

The ATF became a series of micro-agencies and branches where Special Agents in Charge (SACs) built personal law enforcement empires in their divisions, making their own rules and disregarding law, policy, and many times, common sense. That style of management became rampant, and once that tiger was out of the cage, none of the new "cat-tamer" pseudo directors could figure out how to get it back in.

The ATF was viewed internally as a law enforcement *Titanic*: no matter what happened, the leaders felt their ship was unsinkable. Just weather the storms and we'll be fine. A series of short-term directors and even more prevalent temporary "Acting Directors" were imported to "captain" the ship. Then like the *Titanic*, the luxury liner *ATF*, commanded by incompetent captains, hit an iceberg: Fast and Furious.

As has been demonstrated in the ATF Phoenix Field Division, the direction and motivation of the ATF became grossly perverted and tangled in unjust personal philosophies. The ATF's Special Agent in

Charge at the Phoenix Field Division apparently decided that he was going to dictate American policy on gun-related border violence. His incompetence was not just tolerated, it was defended; and when Fast and Furious became an embarrassment, his superiors pretended they were unaware and far from the scene of the crime.

Many people in the ATF saw what was happening and tried to warn the bureau, but the new corrupt and arrogant culture of management had become too powerful and intimidating. Field agents who spoke up were punished for having an opinion and daring to voice it. Whistleblowers had their reputations, careers, and finances shattered. Others of higher ranks knew the wreck was about to happen but dared not open their mouths because they feared doing the right thing might jeopardize a future promotion.

So much has changed. So much of what we once admired in our leadership—in simplest terms, courage and confidence—was replaced by a lack of accountability and a management culture of denial and cover up. There is no place for any person who carries a badge and gun in our country to display the dire lack of testicular fortitude seen recently in the ATF. Ours is not the business for cowards, sissies, or liars.

The ATF is an agency that I will always love, but it has disappointed me and many agents. We are better than this, much better. We have a proud history of standing up against the most violent predators in our communities. Even in the wake of Operations Wide Receiver and Fast and Furious, ATF agents continue to outperform agents from other federal agencies in the per capita production of investigations, operations, arrests, indictments, and prosecutions. The ATF has always been proud to "do more with less," but today the accomplishments of ATF agents are rarely due to our leadership, but more likely, in spite of it.

Once while assisting the DEA on a plan for an undercover operation to buy drugs from a suspect, I spoke up as an ATF agent. "I hope that he shows up high and with a pipe bomb in one pocket and a sawed-off shotgun in the other." You would have thought I had just slit the throat of the family dog. But this is the mentality of true and good ATF agents everywhere. We have jurisdiction to chase explosives, illegal weapons, and drugs, and I simply wanted to have a chance to go against the worst of the worst. That was not bravado. I am nobody's hero. It was the mentality that I had been trained in. I was proud to take the fight to the streets on behalf of the ATF and, more important, on behalf of America's citizens. It is what we do.

The ATF no longer resembles the agency that hired me in 1987. Yes, in some ways the evolution has been a positive one, but in so many critical ways it is worse. I don't believe the cop mentality of my predecessors is gone; it has simply been overrun by executives who lost their way and never cared to find their way back. What we have gained in technology has been offset by a leadership that lost the edge of old school lawmen.

I hope and pray that the media, the American taxpayer, and Congress will combine forces to reform the ATF and restore its professionalism and capability to execute its unique mission, a mission very few seem to understand. We are not anti-gun—we are anti-crime. We are not in the business of prohibiting or punishing law-abiding gun ownership. We are in the business of bringing to justice those criminals who use guns to murder, rape, extort, and deal drugs. It's not the ATF's duty to engage in a debate about the Second Amendment to the Constitution. Our mission is to enforce the law, and that is a mission that everyone should be able to support.

There is a right way and a wrong way for an ATF agent to go about his or her business. Of late, the wrong way has been revealed. Through accountability, oversight, and a restoration of good management, we at the ATF can return to the right way of handling America's business; when we do, we will re-win the faith and trust of the American people.

Rest in Peace, Brian Terry. Your sacrifice to our country is highlighting and changing the way that we in law enforcement conduct ourselves. Every good law enforcement officer out there is grateful for that.

ATF Special Agent Jay Dobyns
February 2012

CHAPTER ONE

A WARRIOR'S DEATH

"I do not fear death, for I have been close enough to it on enough occasions that it no longer concerns me. What I do fear is the loss of my honor, and would rather die fighting than to have it said that I was without courage."

—Poem by Lieutenant Colonel Watt, found on the desk of Border Patrol Agent Brian Terry

Elite Border Patrol Agent Brian Terry's mother, Josephine, was looking forward to her son spending Christmas at home in Michigan for the first time in years. In the early morning of December 15, 2010, her telephone rang. There would be no more thoughts of a happy Christmas.

Instead, the family gathered in Detroit on December 21 for Brian's funeral. Homeland Security Secretary Janet Napolitano, a former governor of Arizona, offered Josephine condolences on behalf of the president for her fallen son.

■ ■ ■ ■ ■

Brian Terry spent the last moments of his life doing his duty. On a chilly December night, forty-five minutes before his shift was scheduled to end, Terry was part of a team of elite border patrol agents converging on Arizona's Peck Canyon, eighteen miles north of the Mexican border.

Vast and intemperate, the southern Arizona desert is one of the most inhospitable areas in the world. Much of the desert can be reached only by aircraft or on foot. The forbidding environment, coupled with a chronic shortage of border security personnel, has made it an ideal route for drug smugglers, illegal immigrants, and human traffickers.

The small towns along southern Arizona's Interstates 10 and 8 between Yuma and Phoenix—Casa Grande, Arizona City, Maricopa, Hidden Valley, Eloy, and Stanfield—used to be ranching and farming communities. Now they are the stash houses, and their small access roads are the smuggling routes, for the Mexican drug cartels. The cartels operate with something close to impunity, and the Arizona farmers who remain in the area must carry weapons, and some wear bulletproof vests to protect themselves.

In south central Arizona, Lieutenant Matthew Thomas of the Pinal County Sheriff Department's SWAT team has seen cartel members become increasingly defiant. "These guys are ready for a confrontation," Thomas told me one afternoon as I joined him on a patrol. "They have no issue directing violence toward law enforcement."

Indeed, some officials believe that border patrol agents are being targeted for assassination by the drug cartels. In addition, deputies like Thomas confront so-called "rip crews," freelance criminals who raid the cartels' traffickers; the victims' bodies are sometimes found months, even years later.

The trafficking of drugs and illegal immigrants across the border is on a massive scale. In 2010, in the Tucson sector alone, nearly 400 tons of marijuana were seized, and 180,000 illegal immigrants were apprehended. One hundred thirty-three people were listed as victims of the undeclared border war. It is assumed that for all the hundreds of tons of drugs that are captured, hundreds of tons more make it across, and for all the hundreds of thousands of illegal immigrants who are caught, hundreds of thousands more evade law enforcement.

Moreover, turf wars between the Mexican cartels have put Arizonans in the crossfire. In one notorious example in 2010, longtime Arizona rancher Robert Krentz was found shot dead, along with his dog, one day after authorities seized nearly 300 pounds of marijuana close to his ranch. His suspected killer fled back to Mexico.[1]

In June 2010, Pinal County Sheriff Paul Babeu declared flatly that parts of Arizona were under the cartels' control. The Department of Homeland Security responded by posting signs along desert routes that stated, "Travel Caution: Smuggling and Illegal Immigration May Be Encountered in This Area." The Obama administration was willing, de facto, to cede control of parts of southern Arizona to Mexican organized crime. Arizona Governor Jan Brewer, standing in front of one of the "Travel Caution" signs, protested that "these signs calling our desert an active drug and human smuggling area . . . [are] eighty miles away from the border and only thirty miles away from Arizona's capital. This is an outrage."[2]

That same month, the U.S. Department of Fish and Wildlife closed 3,500 acres of the Buenos Aires National Wildlife Refuge that stretches into the Arizona desert from the Mexican border. Because of the Mexican drug cartels, the area was deemed too dangerous for tourists.

So by concession of the Obama administration, parts of Arizona are now officially off limits to American citizens. Peck Canyon, just north of the U.S.-Mexico border, near Nogales, Arizona, used to be a safe place for native Arizonans to live, camp, and hunt. Today, however, drug gang shootouts, armed robbery, and other heinous crimes have become nearly common occurrences because of Mexican criminals. Kids don't play alone outside—their parents fear they will be kidnapped—and few adults venture outside without a loaded pistol.[3]

The drug cartels consider southern Arizona a base of operations. They have a vast intelligence network of informers. Spotters sit atop hills and mountains with cell phones and radios, identifying where sheriffs' vehicles and Border Patrol squads are located. In the late hours of December 14, 2010, they spotted Brian Terry.

■　■　■　■　■

Agent Terry understood that the men he might encounter on patrol were not Boy Scouts. In Mexico, cartel members have no problem using roadside IEDs, murdering women, killing children, beheading people, and dissolving their victims' bodies in caustic soda.[4] They also possess an arsenal of weapons that exceeds the small arms inventory of almost any nation in the world.

Brian Terry had joined the United States Marines Corps straight out of high school. After being honorably discharged in 1994, he again held up his hand and swore an oath, this time to serve as a police officer in the Detroit suburbs of Ecorse and Lincoln Park. In 2007, after receiving a degree in criminal justice, Brian joined the U.S. Border Patrol. "He was a strong, competitive, handsome, courageous, funny, and incredibly patriotic American," a cousin recalled. Tall and brawny, Brian still had the bearing of a military man. He cropped his hair close, much as he had in the Marines.

Because of his law enforcement and military background, Brian was recruited for an elite, special operations group of the Border Patrol known as the U.S. Border Patrol Tactical Unit, or by its acronym, BORTAC. Comprised of specialized SWAT teams that undergo grueling training regimens, the agents provide rapid response to emergency situations. They were the only units with the training and expertise to operate in the Arizona wilderness no man's land in the dark of night.

As a trainee, Brian Terry was a standout. He was once told by his instructor that he had done a task incorrectly. The penalty was a three-mile run in the unforgiving heat of the American southwest; and he had to do it while carrying fifty pounds of tactical gear and another recruit across his shoulders. When Brian was one mile into the run, the instructor discovered that he had in fact made the mistake, not Brian. He told Brian he could stop running. Brian refused. "I'll never quit a task until it is finished," he said. It was due to such exploits that his friends and co-workers nicknamed Brian "Superman." He seemed to be able to do anything.

Though Brian and his team routinely wore night vision goggles, they did not need them on December 14. The evening was cloudless, and Peck Canyon was illuminated by the light of a half moon. In the distance, Brian's squad spotted five bandits, each armed with an AK-47 rifle. The agents approached cautiously, near silently, before shouting: "United States Border Patrol! Drop your weapons!" Instead the bandits prepared to fire. As required by Border Patrol regulations, Brian and the other agents fired bean bags as warning shots. Their enemies weren't firing bean bags.

■ ■ ■ ■ ■

What Brian Terry's family did not know, as they tried to cope with the loss of their son during Christmas 2010, was that the AK-47 that had fired the round that killed Brian had been sold to the Mexican drug cartels under the supervision of the United States government, and that the weapon sale was only one deadly part of a terrible scandal overseen by the Obama administration itself, which had intentionally funneled arms to the drug cartels' borderland killers. Josephine Terry, and millions of bewildered Americans who followed the story in the news, were left with one haunting question: Why?

CHAPTER TWO

CLINGING TO THEIR GUNS

*"It's not surprising then they get bitter, they cling to guns
or religion or antipathy to people who aren't like them or
anti-immigrant sentiment or anti-trade sentiment as a
way to explain their frustrations."*

—Barack Obama, April 2008

Only the high-dollar liberal donors gathered in the room were supposed to have heard Barack Obama's now-infamous attack on the people of small-town Pennsylvania. Speaking at a fundraiser in San Francisco on April 6, 2008, the improbable frontrunner in the Democratic presidential primaries tried to explain why midwestern blue-collar voters were not voting for him. True to form, Obama blamed others rather than himself.

"You go into these small towns in Pennsylvania and, like a lot of small towns in the Midwest, the jobs have been gone now for 25 years and nothing's replaced them," Obama said, so people there "get bitter" and "cling to guns or religion."

Obama's off-the-cuff comments stirred outrage. His Democratic opponent Hillary Clinton, though no friend of gun owners herself, denounced Obama's views, saying they "were not reflective of the values and beliefs of Americans."[1] The comments did, however, appear to be reflective of the values and beliefs of Barack Obama.

An antipathy to guns and gun owners is part of Obama's DNA. More than once in his memoir *Dreams from My Father,* Obama refers to "white men," "their guns," and the trouble they bring.[2] Obama recounts stories told by his Kenyan grandmother about "white men who appeared with rifles" and terrorized the African villages of his ancestors.[3]

Even before he sought public office, Barack Obama was on a mission to subvert the Second Amendment and deprive gun owners of their constitutional rights. In law school, he was mentored by liberal legal scholar Laurence H. Tribe, who at the time was a fervent opponent of gun rights. Obama, Tribe recalled, was "the best student I ever had."[4]

In 1994, Obama joined the board of the Joyce Foundation, a liberal-leaning organization so active in advocating restrictions on gun ownership that it is known as "the anti-NRA." Community organizer Obama was also associated with the Independent Voters of Illinois—Independent Precinct Organization,[5] a group that supports "gun control and the right of municipalities to ban sales or possession of handguns and assault weapons." Another director of the group was the Obamas' close friend Valerie Jarrett. Jarrett was deputy chief of staff to Chicago mayor Richard Daley, and was a major supporter of the city's handgun ban.

As a politician in Chicago, Obama racked up a consistent record of supporting restrictions on gun ownership. For instance, in 1999 Obama was quoted by the *Chicago Defender* newspaper at an "anti-gun rally" proposing a 500 percent increase in federal taxes "on the sale of firearm ammunition."[6] In 2000, as an Illinois state senator, Obama co-sponsored legislation to limit law-abiding citizens to the purchase of one handgun a month. In 2003, Obama voted for a bill banning the private ownership of hunting shotguns, target rifles, and black powder rifles in Illinois.[7]

In 2004, the Illinois state legislature passed a law that permitted citizens to defend themselves and others with a gun at their home or business even if local ordinances prohibited gun ownership. The bill came in response to a celebrated case where a father, at home with his children, had shot at a burglar who had broken into their house. Fifty-four-year-old Hale DeMar was charged with violating a local ordinance after shooting a burglar who was in the process of robbing his Chicago-area home. The intruder, a convicted felon named Mario Billings, had entered his house through the kitchen door, tripping an alarm system. Mr. DeMar, a local restaurateur, was in the house at the time with his two young children. When DeMar came across the man attempting to steal a flat-screen computer monitor, he opened fire with a .38-caliber pistol, shooting the burglar in the shoulder. Billings made his way out of the house and into one of DeMar's vehicles and drove himself to a hospital, where he was arrested.

Mr. DeMar was also charged with a crime: violating a local ordinance that prohibited handgun ownership. The action sparked controversy across Illinois. In response, the state legislature passed a law, S.B. 2165, ordering that local gun bans could not be enforced in cases where the gun owner could prove the weapon was being used in self-defense or the defense of another while in his home or place of business. That legislation passed the Illinois State Senate by an overwhelming margin. Barack Obama, then a state senator, voted against the law—twice.[8]

Obama has long believed one of the best solutions to crime prevention is the reinstatement of the Clinton-era assault weapons ban. Despite the politically inflammatory name, guns under the category of "assault weapons" have existed for more than a century and have been used by millions of Americans for target shooting and, in some cases, self-defense. During his campaign for the United States Senate in 2004, Obama called President Bush's refusal to renew the ban a "scandal."[9]

Once in the U.S. Senate, Obama voted against legislation to protect firearms distributors, manufacturers, and local gun dealers from lawsuits for crimes committed with guns and ammunition they lawfully sold.[10] In his second memoir, *The Audacity of Hope*, Obama expanded on his views. "I believe in keeping guns out of our inner cities, and that our leaders must say so in the face of the gun manufacturers' lobby," he wrote.

In his run for the 2008 Democratic presidential nomination, Obama tempered his rhetoric on gun rights, though he still voted to find ways to "stem the flow" of guns by "unscrupulous gun dealers."[11] His campaign website also promised that Obama "will protect the rights of hunters and other law-abiding Americans to purchase, own, transport and use guns."[12] Nonetheless Obama's true views kept finding their way into the headlines.

After Barack Obama's "clinging to their guns" gaffe, the Clinton campaign began sending out fliers in midwestern states accusing Obama of a full-scale assault on Second Amendment rights. The front of the mailing asked the following: "Where does Barack Obama really stand on guns?" The answer was: "Depends on who he is talking to."

The mailer cited Obama's support for a complete ban on handguns when he was a candidate for the state Senate in 1996, citing a questionnaire Candidate Obama signed to win the endorsement of the Independent Voters of Illinois—Independent Precinct Organization.

Obama responded to the charge the same way he has responded to similar charges since he became president: with scapegoating, evasiveness, and outright falsehoods.

First, he claimed that he never "saw or approved" the questionnaire—someone on his staff had approved it without consulting him, though the original copy had his handwriting on it.[13] At an ABC News-hosted debate between Hillary Clinton and Obama in Philadelphia on April 16, 2008, moderator Charlie Gibson and Obama had the following exchange:

> **Gibson:** And in 1996, your campaign issued a questionnaire, and your writing was on the questionnaire that said you favored a ban on handguns.

> **Obama:** No, my writing wasn't on that particular questionnaire, Charlie. As I said, I have never favored an all-out ban on handguns.

After that remark, the website FactCheck.org, established by the left-leaning Annenberg Public Policy Center, reported that Obama "was wrong about that—his handwriting appears on a small part of the document—but he has continued to maintain that a campaign aide filled out the bulk of it, including the multipart question asking if he supported state legislation to ban assault weapons; ban manufacture, sale and possession of handguns; and require waiting periods and back-ground checks before gun purchases. He answered 'Yes' on all counts."[14]

On March 31, 2008, *Politico* shed additional light on the situation. "Obama played a greater role than his aides now acknowledge in craft-ing liberal stands on gun control, the death penalty and abortion—positions that appear at odds with the more moderate image he has projected during his presidential campaign," the online political site reported after talking to sources close to Obama. The story went on to charge that not only had Obama been interviewed about the issues in the questionnaire, he had actually amended some of his answers.

According to the *Politico* story, Obama's protests of ignorance were "galling" to "many members" of the Independent Voters of Illinois—Independent Precinct Organization. Some members of the board argued that Obama's 1996 answers were "what he really believes in, and he's tailoring it now to make himself more palatable as a nation-wide candidate." Several dismissed Obama's claim that he had never seen the questionnaire as "ridiculous."[15]

Asked at a Democratic debate if he still favored the registration and licensing of guns, Obama said he did believe in some limits on gun ownership, and added: "We can trace guns that have been used in crimes to unscrupulous gun dealers that may be selling to straw pur-chasers and dumping them on the streets."[16] Those words would take on new meaning once he was president.

■ ■ ■ ■ ■

Within a month of his general election victory over Republican John McCain, President-elect Obama selected Eric Holder as attorney general of the United States. Holder and Obama had been friends since 2004, after meeting at a dinner party. "We just clicked," Holder said later.[17] The future attorney general was a campaign co-chairman for Obama's presidential race, acting as a fundraiser and prominent surrogate. At 6' 3", Holder had been a high school basketball player. Even at age fifty-seven, he was one of the few who could mount a challenge to Obama on the court. He was a voracious reader, and said he found no book more inspiring than the autobiography of Malcolm X.[18] As a freshman at Columbia in 1969, Holder and several other students took over the campus's ROTC office and turned it into a student center named after his adolescent idol.

In 1999, as a Justice Department official in the Clinton administration, Holder sought to fast-track clemency for sixteen Puerto Rican FALN (Armed Forces of National Liberation) terrorists responsible for more than 130 bombings, which had killed four Americans and wounded eighty more. Over the opposition of the FBI, U.S. attorneys, police organizations, and the families of the victims, Holder arranged for their sentences to be commuted.[19]

As a deputy attorney general in Janet Reno's Clinton-era Justice Department, Holder backed the assault weapons ban and defended the department's bungled attack on the Branch Davidian compound in Waco, Texas, in 1993. In 1999, the Clinton administration plotted to curtail gun rights and "to prepare an all-out offensive on guns in the coming year," as one senior White House aide put it.[20] Eric Holder was one of the most vocal proponents of the plan. He favored requiring safety locks for all guns, gun-buyer background checks, and a strenuous certification process for all handgun owners.[21] In a 1999 interview, ABC News asked Mr. Holder whether the Second Amendment recognizes "that citizens have a right to bear arms," including the right to "buy a firearm?" Holder responded, "No court has ever said that the Second Amendment actually says that. I think, if you look at it, it talks about bearing guns in a well regulated militia. And I don't think anywhere it talks about an individual."

After his service in the Clinton administration—including his controversial role in helping arrange a presidential pardon for Marc Rich, a disgraced financier and friend of the Clintons, who had been on the FBI's top ten most wanted list for years for tax evasion and making business deals with the Iranians during the Iranian hostage crisis[22]—Holder became a prominent Washington, D.C., attorney in private practice. After the September 11, 2001, terrorist attacks, Holder urged Democrats to enact sweeping gun laws. "To increase security at home," he wrote that a necessary measure would be "background checks on all gun sales." Holder added: "Congress should also pass legislation that would give the Bureau of Alcohol, Tobacco and Firearms a record of every firearm sale."

One year before Obama's election, Holder joined an amicus brief with Janet Reno defending Washington, D.C., against a resident challenging the city's ban on guns. Although the Supreme Court overturned the ban and rejected Holder's arguments, Holder insisted that the Virginia Tech and Columbine school massacres proved "the deadly toll that firearms exact" and were evidence enough that the Second Amendment should be read as a collective, not an individual, right.[23]

■ ■ ■ ■ ■

The same day President-elect Obama chose Holder as his attorney general, he also nominated Arizona governor Janet Napolitano as Secretary of Homeland Security. Like Holder, Napolitano was an early endorser of Obama's presidential bid. Napolitano was a former attorney general for the state of Arizona. In that role, she had repeatedly blasted the federal government for its inattention to border issues. Running for governor in a Republican-leaning state, Napolitano claimed she was a supporter of Second Amendment rights and if elected had no intention to seek new gun control legislation.

Once elected, Napolitano vetoed legislation that would have guaranteed the right of a law-abiding citizen to confront a criminal with a firearm. The bill was meant to correct a quirk in Arizona law, which allowed a citizen to fire at a criminal in justifiable self-defense only as long as the citizen drew and fired right away; merely drawing a gun and pointing it at a criminal could lead to prosecution. But this commonsense fix was opposed by the anti-gun lobby. She also vetoed a bill that would have made concealed carry permits valid for the lifetime of the holder. As governor, she worked with Mexico on a gun-tracing program called "eTrace," designed to find out where guns found in Mexico had originated and whether they had been purchased in her state.[24]

Napolitano was not considered controversial, and her confirmation as Secretary of Homeland Security proceeded smoothly. Holder's nomination was a different story, given his reputation as a fiercely partisan member of the Bill Clinton-era Justice Department. During confirmation hearings, Holder admitted to "mistakes" in the pardon of fugitive financier Marc Rich—mistakes that he claimed were "not typical" of his conduct.[25]

Mr. Holder's views on guns were another lively topic during his confirmation. In a January 2009 letter to Senate Judiciary Committee chairmen Patrick Leahy and Arlen Specter, the National Rifle Association accused Holder of supporting extremely restrictive gun control laws. The letter cited Holder's support for the Clinton-era assault rifle ban, a three-day waiting period on the purchase of handguns, an increase in the age requirement for handgun possession, holding adults responsible for juvenile gun offenses, a limit on the number of handguns one could purchase in a month, and a burdensome requirement for firearms dealers to make monthly reports to the Bureau of Alcohol, Tobacco, Firearms, and Explosives (ATF), which some feared would lead to all firearms having to be registered with the federal government.[26] Holder's views on the Second Amendment were troubling enough that twenty-one Republican senators voted against his confirmation.

■　■　■　■　■

Bipartisan support for Janet Napolitano as Secretary of Homeland Security dissolved when a nine-page Department of Homeland Security report on the dangers of "rightwing extremism" became public. The report, an unclassified assessment sent to law enforcement agencies across the country, was entitled "Rightwing Extremism: Current Economic and Political Climate Fueling Resurgence in Radicalization and Recruitment."

Though the report said it had "no specific information that domestic rightwing terrorists are currently planning acts of violence," it said the faltering economy could incite such groups. Of particular note was the report's definition of rightwing extremism. It listed "those that are mainly antigovernment, rejecting federal authority in favor of state or local authority, or rejecting government authority entirely." Likely sources of rightwing extremism, according to the report, were disgruntled veterans of the Iraq and Afghanistan wars, abortion opponents, and gun owners.[27]

Secretary Napolitano refused to repudiate the report when given the opportunity.

"Let me be very clear: we monitor the risks of violent extremism taking root here in the United States," she said in a statement. "We don't have the luxury of focusing our efforts on one group; we must protect the country from terrorism whether foreign or homegrown, and regardless of the ideology that motivates its violence."[28]

Days later, Napolitano had a change in heart, seeming particularly determined to ease the offense the report had caused among veterans' groups. In a statement issued by the Department after a meeting with a veterans' group leader, Napolitano stated, "We connected meaningfully about the important issues that have emerged over recent days, and I offered him my sincere apologies for any offense to our veterans caused by this report....I pledge that the department has fixed the internal process that allowed this document to be released before it was ready."[29]

In February 2009, days after being confirmed by the U.S. Senate, Holder appeared at a press conference to claim credit for a crackdown on Mexican drug cartels through an operation overseen by the Justice Department and Drug Enforcement Agency. "The Department of Justice under my leadership will continue to work with our counterparts in Mexico, through information sharing, training and mutual cooperation to jointly fight these cartels, both in Mexico and the United States," Holder said.

The new attorney general also announced plans to re-instate the assault weapons ban. Holder claimed the re-instatement of the ban would, at a minimum, have a positive impact in Mexico. "As President Obama indicated during the campaign, there are just a few gun-related changes that we would like to make," Holder said.[30] Unbeknownst to the country, a plot to implement these "few changes" was already in its early stages.

CHAPTER THREE

ORIGINS OF A SCANDAL

> *"The president has directed us to take action to fight these cartels and Attorney General Eric Holder and I are taking several new and aggressive steps as part of the administration's comprehensive plan."*
>
> —Deputy Attorney General David Ogden, February 24, 2009

> *"[W]e monitored as [cartel members] purchased hand guns, AK-47 variants, and .50 caliber rifles almost daily.... Knowing all the while, just days after these purchases, the guns that we saw these individuals buy would begin turning up at crime scenes in the United States and Mexico, we still did nothing."*
>
> —ATF whistleblower Special Agent John Dodson, June 15, 2011

On March 24, 2009, two months after Obama's inauguration, Deputy Attorney General David Ogden appeared before television cameras in the basement of the West Wing. Ogden was another early and controversial Obama appointee to the Justice Department, a former ACLU attorney criticized by conservative groups for his opposition to Internet filtering sites to block child pornography[1] and for opposing parental consent laws for underage girls seeking abortions.[2] "You've taken some very extraordinary positions, some left-leaning and unorthodox positions," Arizona Senator Jon Kyl told Ogden during confirmation hearings.[3]

Perhaps it was because he was new to the job—he had been confirmed by the Senate only twelve days earlier—or perhaps it was the White House press corps arrayed in front of him, but Ogden appeared nervous, even shaking, as he spoke at his first major press conference.[4]

The subject of his remarks was an initiative which Ogden said was being launched at the express direction of the president of the United States. Referencing the rise in arms trafficking from Mexican gangs into the United States, Ogden reported, "The president has directed us to take action to fight these cartels and Attorney General Eric Holder and I are taking several new and aggressive steps as part of the administration's comprehensive plan."[5]

Ogden announced an expansion of an ATF initiative known as Project Gunrunner, which had begun in 2005 as a pilot project in Laredo, Texas. The program aimed at arresting illegal "straw" purchasers—individuals who buy weapons on behalf of others—to help stem the flow of guns going to the cartels. The Obama administration intended to extend the Bush-era project across the American southwest. At the heart of the expansion was a reinvigorated effort to trace guns through an ATF system known as eTrace, a program Napolitano had also championed in Arizona. The eTrace system enables law enforcement agents to track the serial numbers of guns found at crime scenes to their point of purchase.

As highlighted by the administration, Project Gunrunner became a major priority, involving multiple government agencies and departments, including the ATF and FBI, both under Holder's Justice Department, and the Border Patrol, under Napolitano's Department of Homeland Security.

The president directed all relevant departments and agencies to conduct a top-to-bottom review of their gun policies. The Justice Department developed new anti-gun-trafficking squads to be stationed along the Southwest Border, while the Department of Homeland Security ensured that its Immigration and Customs Enforcement Agency (ICE) shared information and resources on gun trafficking investigations. The Obama administration was indeed confronting a legitimate problem. Since 2006, 48,000 people had been murdered in the cartel wars in Mexico.[6] But it was not long before the Obama administration's top officials took aim at those they believed were the real culprits behind the Mexican violence: American gun owners. In the aftermath of the "Fast and Furious" scandal, administration officials repeatedly denied that their activities were motivated by an effort to curtail Second Amendment rights, but what they said when the initiative was launched was rather different: they implied that American gun shops were the source of the problem.

■　■　■　■　■

The day after the Justice Department announcement, Homeland Security Secretary Janet Napolitano drove down Massachusetts Avenue from her office to Capitol Hill, where she pledged her department's full support for the new initiative. "A large number of weapons recovered in Mexico's drug war are smuggled illegally into Mexico from the United States," Napolitano said in testimony before the Senate Judiciary Committee in May 2009. "Clearly, stopping this flow must be an urgent priority."[7]

Shortly thereafter the newly installed Secretary of State, Hillary Clinton, traveled to Mexico, where, in an interview with MSNBC's Andrea Mitchell, she went out of her way to note, "We're going to start tracing these guns, we're going to start cracking down on illegal gun sales, we're going to go after the straw men and women who go in and buy these guns," she said. "We're going to use every tool at our disposal."[8] It was a rare foray into domestic policy for the nation's top diplomat.

Clinton also laid blame for the gun trafficking on U.S. gun shop owners. "The guns that are used by the drug cartels against the police and the military—90 percent of them come from America," she charged. "Our inability to prevent weapons from being illegally smuggled across the border to arm these criminals causes the deaths of police officers, soldiers, civilians, so yes I feel very responsible."[9]

Only a week after the Clinton visit, Attorney General Holder traveled to Cuernavaca, Mexico, where he promoted Project Gunrunner as "a major new effort to break the backs of the cartels."[10]

Holder too spoke about the urgent need to stop the supposed flow of thousands of guns—he called it an "iron river"—from U.S. gun shops to the cartels in Mexico.[11]

On April 16, 2009, President Obama himself traveled to Mexico City. At a joint press conference with Mexican President Felipe Calderon, Obama reiterated that he had personally ordered an overhaul of all operations targeting Mexican cartel weapons and drug trafficking. "In fact, I've asked Eric Holder to do a complete review of how our current enforcement operations are working and make sure we are cutting down on the loopholes that are causing some of these drug trafficking problems," the president said.

In addition to reaffirming his belief that the assault weapons ban should be reinstated in order to "prevent" gun trafficking to Mexico, the president had another idea he wanted to highlight. "Last point I would make is that there are going to be some opportunities where I think we can build some strong consensus," Obama said. "I'll give you one example and that is the issue of gun tracing, the tracing of bullets and ballistics and gun information that had been used in major crimes."[12]

Standing beside Obama, President Calderon used the press conference to finger the usual culprits for the violence besieging his country. Not the drug cartels making billions from the sale of heroin, cocaine, amphetamines, and other drugs they transport into the United States. Not the corrupt Mexican police or border control personnel or national, state, and local politicians taking bribes to look the other way. Like Obama, the Mexican president believed the real culprits were U.S. gun shops.

"This war is being waged with guns purchased not here, but in the United States," Calderon said. Echoing Hillary Clinton's remarks from her visit a few months earlier, he added, "More than 90 percent of the guns recovered in Mexico come from the United States, many from gun shops that line our shared border."

The facts are quite different. For one thing, the Mexican government does a poor job of tracing guns in general; it doesn't know where most of the recovered crime-linked guns originate. And the "90 percent" statistic—cited by American liberals for years—does not appear to be accurate. In 2009, for example, 21,313 guns were recovered in Mexico and submitted for tracing. Only 5,444, or 25 percent, were sourced to U.S. gun dealers.[13]

During the WikiLeaks controversy, a confidential State Department cable, dated October 29, 2010, and labeled "09Mexico 3114 Mexico Arms Trafficking: Access to Confiscated," was leaked to the public.[14] The cable, sent to the State Department by the U.S. ambassador in Mexico, stated the following: "Claims by Mexican and U.S. officials that upwards of 90 percent of illegal recovered weapons can be traced back to the U.S. is based on an incomplete survey of confiscated weapons. In point of fact, without wider access to the weapons seized in Mexico, we really have no way of verifying these numbers."[15]

Many of the American guns in Mexico come not from gun shops, but from the U.S. State Department itself, through arms sales to the Mexican military.[16] A large fraction of these guns eventually end up "lost" and in the hands of cartels. The cartels get most of their weapons from corrupt Mexican military personnel,[17] from leftover military stockpiles in Central America,[18] specifically El Salvador, and from cheap non-American sources like China.[19]

Regardless of the actual facts, it was clear the Obama administration was united in its enmity toward American gun shop owners. Close them down, as NRA President David Keene says, and you close down the Second Amendment. After all, he maintained, what good is the right to own firearms if there is no place to purchase them?

■ ■ ■ ■ ■

With a revamped Project Gunrunner that boasted a presidential imprimatur, additional authority, and expanded resources, including a new database for gun tracing, the ATF sought to make inroads against the Mexican cartels besieging the border. If, in the process, the bureau could prove that U.S. guns were fueling the violence, and that the vast majority of guns found at grisly cartel-related crime scenes could be traced to American gun shops, all the better. The Department of Justice chose Phoenix, Arizona, and the ATF's field office there to begin its offensive against the drug cartels. They dubbed the plan "Operation Fast and Furious."

The curious name derived from a 2001 Hollywood film about gangsters stealing and racing cars. The cover of an official ATF slide-show presentation from spring 2010 proudly displays a logo from the film and a photo of a street-racing car. The unofficial name wasn't outlined in the ATF or Justice Department budget, which kept the operation hidden under the broader Project Gunrunner program.

The agency at the center of "Fast and Furious," the Bureau of Alcohol, Tobacco, Firearms and Explosives (ATF), has had a checkered history. Though its agents were once known as "the Cowboys" for their daring exploits, the agency has been plagued for decades by leadership problems and mishandled cases. In 1992, the bureau played a pivotal role in the investigation of Randy Weaver leading to the controversial shootout at Ruby Ridge, Idaho, which took the lives of a U.S. marshal, a woman, and a child. One year later, an ATF siege against the Branch Davidian religious group near Waco, Texas, ended in a gun battle and the fiery deaths of seventy-six people, including twenty children and sect leader David Koresh. In 1995, *Time* magazine described the bureau as "the most-hated federal agency in America."[20]

To reduce criticism, the bureau was moved from the Treasury Department to the Justice Department in 2003. Still, a 2006 Inspector General Office's report found the ATF continued to be rife with mismanagement and employee grievances. One of the most notorious cases of mismanagement involved the ATF field office in Phoenix. ATF Special Agent Jay Dobyns had been the first federal agent to successfully infiltrate multiple layers of the Hells Angels gang through "Operation Black Biscuit." With a goatee, skull rings on each of his fingers, tattoos covering his biceps and forearms, and rarely without his bandana or sunglasses, the 6' 2" former University of Arizona wide receiver blended flawlessly into America's most notorious motorcycle gang.

Having nearly single handedly brought down the Hells Angels, and locking away dozens of its members, Dobyns had a target on his back. The Hells Angels wanted him dead.

In 2004, Dobyns and ATF became aware of credible violent threats against him and his family. They included plans to murder him by injecting him with the AIDS virus, kidnapping and torturing his then fifteen-year-old daughter, and kidnapping his wife in order to videotape a gang rape of her.

The ATF learned that Hells Angels had solicited contracts with the Aryan Brotherhood and the MS-13 gang to carry out these threats, which were laid out in prison letters and confirmed through interviews of confidential informants in prison. Dobyns was at the top of an Aryan Brotherhood hit list. "Permission to kill" had been granted.[21]

Dobyns maintains that he reported these threats to the Special Agent in Charge at the Phoenix field office—a man named Bill Newell—and asked for protection for his family. Perhaps feeling the claims were insubstantial, Newell refused to take any countermeasures to protect his agent. Dobyns himself has no explanation for what he saw as Newell's inexplicable decision.

Newell had earned a reputation for punishing those who questioned his authority. When Dobyns pointed out to others his boss's failure to address violent death threats against a federal agent, Newell retaliated. Though Newell could not fire him outright, he could make Dobyns' time in Arizona a living hell.

Soon after the threats had been reported to Newell and the ATF, Dobyns' house was set on fire at 3:00 a.m. His family was sleeping inside. They managed to escape, but the intimidation had taken a dangerous turn.

Newell doubled down. He had subordinates accuse Dobyns of purposely burning down his own home for attention and named Dobyns as a suspect. The effort to frame Dobyns was unsuccessful, and his vindictive treatment by Newell and his associates was reported to ATF headquarters in Washington.

A subsequent Department of Justice inspector general report later concluded that management within the ATF Phoenix office, despite having the necessary resources, did not adequately address threats made against Dobyns. It found "absence of any corrective measures proposed to address the failure to conduct timely and thorough investigations into the death threats made against Dobyns."[22] A separate U.S. Office of Special Counsel report concluded, "I note with concern the absence of any corrective measures proposed to address the failure to conduct timely and thorough investigations into the death threats made against Special Agent Dobyns. ATF does not appear to have held anyone accountable in this regard."[23]

Bill Newell was neither reprimanded nor removed from his post. He remained the head of the Phoenix ATF office when President Obama assumed office.

"ATF today is not anything that the agency that hired me twenty-five years ago was," Dobyns recalled during an interview.[24]

While previous administrators of the agency had been police officers and investigators at heart, Dobyns reflected, they had gradually been replaced by bureaucrats, politicized bureaucrats at that. "These people have come to believe that they somehow are allowed to affect the policy of America by the way they administer the agency and enforce gun laws," he said. "When I came on the job, ATF wasn't about gun control. It was about enforcing the federal firearms laws. And now the agency is about denying honest people their Second Amendment rights."[25]

ATF Agent Peter Forcelli was transferred from New York to become a Group Supervisor of the Phoenix field office in 2007. Forcelli, a law enforcement veteran of twenty-five years experience, had begun his career as a New York City cop and detective where he responded to more than six hundred homicide scenes. When the Twin Towers came crashing down on September 11, 2001, Forcelli helped recover the bodies of the policemen and firefighters he had served alongside.

"It was a mind blowing experience coming to Arizona," Forcelli told me. "ATF didn't do Bill Newell any favors by making him a Special Agent in Charge," he added. "Bill Newell spent almost no time in the field."[26] Newell's lack of field experience was a familiar complaint among ATF agents. Yet, as the senior agent in the ATF's Phoenix field office, Newell was placed at the helm of operation "Fast and Furious."

Newell and his deputy, George Gillett, were odd men to put—or at least keep—in charge of anything. ATF had already had to pay out more than a million dollars in ethics complaint settlements on behalf of Newell, and Gillett had been the subject of a number of disciplinary actions. Agents complained about his incompetence and mismanagement.

Where Gillett excelled, agents claimed, was as Newell's hatchet man—he was the guy who got things done for the boss.[27]

Working closely with the ATF field office on the "Fast and Furious" case was the senior federal prosecutor in the state of Arizona, U.S. Attorney Dennis Burke. Mr. Burke was well-known in the state as a "crony" of Janet Napolitano and was said to wear his political ambitions on his sleeve. Napolitano's critics had lodged many complaints about her efforts to promote Burke for political office.[28]

Before Napolitano became governor, she served as Arizona Attorney General, where Burke worked as her chief deputy and special assistant for four years. Burke then served as Napolitano's top aide for five years, while she was governor of Arizona. President Obama named Burke U.S. attorney in 2009. Burke followed Napolitano into the Obama administration, serving as her top Homeland Security advisor in 2009.

Now that he was a federal prosecutor, Burke reported to Eric Holder and the Justice Department, but few doubted that he was in regular contact with Janet Napolitano about law enforcement operations along the border, state politics, and his own outsized ambitions.

Mr. Burke, originally from Chicago, also had ties to President Obama's then chief of staff—the former Chicago congressman Rahm Emanuel. As hard-charging as he was partisan, Emanuel had been a major figure in the Clinton administration. Known for a "break them at the knee caps" mentality toward political opponents, Emanuel was also in favor of restricting Second Amendment rights. Today, as mayor of Chicago, he is a member of Mayors Against Illegal Guns, an anti-Second Amendment group which blames U.S. gun shops for Mexican drug cartel violence.[29]

Emanuel and Burke had worked together in the 1990s to draft the Clinton assault weapons ban. Burke had donated $500 to Emanuel's congressional campaign in 2002, as well as $2,000 for Obama's 2008 presidential bid. While acting as a U.S. attorney, Burke advised Holder on policy and management, especially on border issues, as chairman of the Attorney General's Advisory Committee.

Another Washington-based advisor on Fast and Furious was Lanny Breuer. As a White House counsel, Breuer had defended President Bill Clinton when he was investigated by the Independent Counsel and during the impeachment hearings. Later, he and Eric Holder had become close friends as partners at the Washington law firm of Covington & Burling, where they approved the firm's largest pro bono legal work: the defense of terrorists held at Guantanamo Bay. When Eric Holder became attorney general, he brought Lanny Breuer with him to act as his right hand man. As Holder's confidante, Breuer was given vast authority within the Justice Department, including oversight of Fast and Furious. And as the official who approved federal wiretaps, he would be knowledgeable about its details and essential to the operation's execution.

Thus many of the key players in the Fast and Furious scandal— those in Phoenix directly overseeing operations, such as Burke, and those in Washington overseeing the overseers, such as Holder, Breuer, Emanuel, and Napolitano—had longstanding relationships, similar political views, and favored restricting Second Amendment rights. They put a sensitive, high-priority gun trafficking operation into the hands of an ATF office known for mismanagement and ethical problems.

On October 26, 2009, top officials—including U.S. Attorney Dennis Burke, FBI Director Robert Mueller, leaders of the Drug Enforcement Agency and ATF, and Assistant Attorney General of the Criminal Division Lanny Breuer—were on a conference call to talk about the plans for expanding Project Gunrunner. "Given the national scope of this issue, merely seizing firearms through interdiction will not stop firearms trafficking to Mexico," the meeting agenda stated. "We must identify, investigate, and eliminate the sources of illegally trafficked firearms and the networks that transport them."[30] What this meant was ATF management was going to make a radical departure from the initial goals of Project Gunrunner. Instead of stopping guns from going from the United States to Mexico, the federal government intended to encourage law-abiding gun dealers to sell weapons to suspected Mexican gun traffickers and allow the guns to be trafficked into Mexico. With each sale, the ATF leadership claimed it would gain information and intelligence leads to the "big fish," the upper circle of leadership in the Mexican cartels.

■ ■ ■ ■ ■

In December 2009, ATF agent John Dodson arrived in Phoenix as part of Obama's new Southwest Border Initiative. Quiet, tall, and blue-eyed with brown hair, Dodson had grown up in Virginia. Still the southern gentleman with the manners his parents insisted he uphold, Dodson appends a "ma'am" and "sir" to most sentences.[31]

Dodson had been a Virginia patrol officer for almost a decade before he joined the ATF. He switched from state to federal law enforcement because he enjoyed investigating big cases, and didn't like having them taken away by federal law enforcement officials asserting federal jurisdiction. With the ATF, Dodson was himself a federal agent, now with more than nine years' experience, working on cases with a national impact. His focus in the ATF was on narcotics and weapons trafficking, and he had appeared in court on numerous occasions as an expert witness.

The lead case agent for Fast and Furious in Phoenix, Hope MacAllister, handed Dodson a list of forty-five names of suspected straw purchasers who would be visiting local gun shops and trying to purchase weapons for cartel members. The idea of the operation, Dodson was told, was to conduct surveillance on known straw purchasers for Mexican drug cartels. Dodson was not to interfere as they bought hundreds of high-powered rifles, including .50 caliber sniper rifles, AK-47s, .38 caliber revolvers, and FN Five-seveN® handguns. These guns would then be allowed to "walk" over the border into Mexico, straight into the hands of ruthless criminals.

Agents like Dodson could follow suspects' cars, but never pull them over. The agents could watch known straw purchasers on video, they could use the phone to encourage gun shop employees to make sales, they could use wiretaps on cell phones, but they could never surveil text messaging, even though texting was the main form of communication between cartel members and straw purchasers.[32]

Dodson was shocked by the details of Operation Fast and Furious; it went against every technique and principle of law enforcement with which he was familiar. In his previous experience, "Whenever a 'walk situation' with a gun occurred, nobody went home until we found it, until we got it back," Dodson later recalled. "There were no ifs, ands, or buts." If agents lost their personal weapon, under normal ATF procedures, they risked termination.

"Prior to my coming to Phoenix, Arizona...I never witnessed a situation where there wasn't at least an attempt to interdict or take the firearm at some point," another Special Agent, Larry Alt, recalled.[33]

Allowing guns to "walk," knowingly providing weapons to criminal suspects and attempting to trace them later, had been tried by the Justice Department before, in "Operation Wide Receiver," launched by the Bush administration in 2005 in close cooperation with the Mexican government. In that operation, straw purchasers were closely monitored in the hopes they might lead to others. Some were arrested before they crossed the border back into Mexico. The ones who crossed the border were to be arrested by the Mexican government. When it was discovered that at least four hundred guns were not recovered by authorities and lost in Mexico, the operation was terminated. What the Obama administration was attempting now was a reprisal of a failed operation, but with two twists: no attempt would be made to recover the guns as they crossed the Mexican border, and, as Dodson soon learned, the Mexican government had been kept in the dark about Fast and Furious. Dodson wondered as well why the forty-five straw purchasers on the list handed to him by MacAllister had not been arrested; in his judgment the ATF already had enough evidence against them.

One of the men on that list was Uriel Patino, who had been identified as a straw purchasing suspect as early as October 31, 2009. Patino, investigators soon learned, was among the most notorious on their list, a man whose weapons purchases lacked any effort at subterfuge. Patino was enrolled in the food stamp program, yet he was spending thousands of dollars on weapons.

Patino roped his roommate Jaime Avila into the business. Avila, a short and chubby Hispanic man with a thin mustache, was taken to a gun shop at the end of November 2009, where he and Patino bought weapons together. Dodson and his teammates watched these activities from parking lots in unmarked vehicles and on live video feed. Time after time they witnessed Avila and Patino walk into gun shops with wads of cash and come out bristling with semi-automatic rifles, each gun at a cost of at least $600. Under direct orders from their ATF superiors, Dodson and his fellow agents did not stop them.

■ ■ ■ ■

Fast and Furious was closely followed by Department of Justice officials. On multiple occasions, U.S. Attorney Dennis Burke met with Phoenix ATF Director Bill Newell to discuss the progress of the Fast and Furious operation.[34] "There were DOJ attorneys and prosecutors who were involved in this since the beginning, giving advice," ATF Special Agent Peter Forcelli later revealed.[35]

Burke and his deputy, Assistant U.S. Attorney Emory Hurley, urged ATF agents to continue monitoring and gathering evidence about straw purchasers like Avila. They also made clear that no arrests of these individuals were imminent. Between 2009 and 2011, Burke and Hurley refused to prosecute nearly every "straw purchaser" case handed to them, citing "no probable cause."[36] On numerous occasions, Hurley personally stopped ATF agents from interdicting weapons. Lower-level prosecutors in the Arizona U.S. Attorney's Office wanted to do good work, but they were suppressed by Burke and Hurley. Once suspects crossed into Mexico (and outside U.S. jurisdiction) with these guns, cases were dropped altogether.[37] "In their opinion, the gun being in Mexico meant the evidence of the crime was in Mexico," Forcelli said. "For two years, if the gun went to Mexico, that case was dead."

While Fast and Furious was underway, Burke took opportunities to denounce gun shop owners. During a news conference in 2010, the U.S. attorney complained about guns being sold in Arizona that were being found in Mexico. "We have a huge problem here," he said. "We have now become the gun locker of the Mexican drug cartels." He did not add that his office and the ATF were at that very moment letting cartel figures help themselves to U.S. guns.[38]

Even today Forcelli remains baffled by the U.S. attorney's actions. "[U.S. Attorney] Emory [Hurley] shat on a couple other significant cases we were working on, including a case on grenades," Forcelli says. In the grenade case, a suspect named Jean Baptiste Kingery was believed by Forcelli and other agents to be sending grenades out of the country, trafficking parts for grenades into Mexico, and then building the explosives for the cartels.

"Their advice was, under no circumstances, do not let him leave the country but, if you catch him leaving the country, we won't prosecute him," Forcelli explains. "They tied our hands."[39]

Eventually, Kingery was arrested by ATF agents as he tried to cross into Mexico with grenade parts and components packed in his tires. Forcelli received a full-blown confession from Kingery. The suspect reportedly admitted that he had been making grenades for the cartels and smuggling explosives across an international border. Instead of a prosecution from Burke or Hurley, they dismissed the case and Kingery went free.

"The only hands the U.S. Attorney's Office handcuffed in the Kingery case were the hands of ATF," Forcelli recalls.[40] He could offer no explanation for these unusual events.

"In my opinion, dozens of firearms traffickers were given a pass by the U.S. Attorney's Office for the District of Arizona," Forcelli says today. "Despite the existence of 'probable cause' in many cases, there were no indictments, no prosecutions, and criminals were allowed to walk free. In short, their office policies, in my opinion, helped pave a dangerous path."[41]

In another instance, the Arizona U.S. Attorney's Office dismissed charges against gun trafficker Fidel Hernandez, who had been purchasing dozens of weapons to be used in cartel murders south of the border.[42] Some of the most basic law enforcement techniques—search and seizure warrants and civil forfeitures—were withheld from agents by Hurley. He required ATF agents to meet extremely strict evidentiary standards to even speak with suspects.[43] Proffers (agreements that give criminal suspects some legal protection in exchange for their testimony) and standard law enforcement inquiries weren't allowed.[44] "We didn't have those tools available to us in Arizona because the United States Attorney's Office wouldn't allow us to utilize waivers of speedy presentment [similar to an indictment] before a magistrate, proffers almost never happened, the basic investigative techniques that I used with great success in the southern district of New York [and] eastern district in New York weren't being deployed in the district in Arizona," Forcelli said.[45]

An ATF briefing paper, dated January 8, 2010, about John Dodson's new ATF unit (the Phoenix Group VII gunrunner strike force) tasked with implementing Fast and Furious, further demonstrated that the U.S. Attorney's Office in Phoenix was well aware that hundreds of guns were being illegally purchased: "Currently our strategy is to allow the transfer of firearms to continue to take place, albeit at a much slower pace, in order to further the investigation and allow for identification of additional co-conspirators who continue to operate illegally to traffic firearms to Mexican DTOs [drug trafficking organizations] which are perpetrating armed violence long the Southwest Border," the paper stated. "This investigation was briefed to United States Attorney Dennis Burke, who concurs with the assessment of his line prosecutors and fully supports the continuation of this investigation. Furthermore, Phoenix Special Agent in Charge Newell has repeatedly met with USA [U.S. attorney] Burke regarding the on-going status of this investigation and both are in full agreement with the current investigative strategy."[46]

But the gun flow from the United States to Mexico wasn't continuing at a slower pace, it was speeding up.

■　■　■　■　■

The Lone Wolf Trading Company sits in a Glendale, Arizona, strip mall, indistinguishable from the dozens of others between Route 17 and the Agua Fria Freeway. Wedged beside a Sprouts grocery store, Lone Wolf's front room is no more than 2,500 square feet. On display is a wide variety of semi-automatic pistols, rifles, and Second Amendment gear—t-shirts, hats, and accessories printed with images of American flags, eagles, and guns. Model airplanes and helicopters hang from the ceiling, and the walls are decorated with hunting trophy animal heads. The ATF used small gun shops like Lone Wolf in Operation Fast and Furious.

Lone Wolf's owner, Andre Howard, has been in the gun-dealing business for twenty-one years, though the former Army pilot doesn't own a gun, rarely hunts, and takes more interest in his other business of giving flying lessons.[47]

In September 2009, Hope MacAllister, flashing a badge indentifying her as an agent with the Phoenix ATF, entered the store. Gun shop owners have reason to view the ATF with some trepidation, because the agency plays a prominent role in determining which gun shop owners keep their licenses.

MacAllister told Howard it was his duty to help the federal government's investigations against the Mexican drug cartels. She told him to expect a big jump in sales, and requested that ATF agents be allowed to tap the shop's telephones and install hidden cameras.[48]

Mr. Howard agreed to cooperate with MacAllister. For fifteen months, he sold guns as directed by her and other ATF agents. Repeatedly, Howard was told to ignore the red flags of illegal gun purchasers: blatantly forged identification, large payments in cash, and interest in bulk purchases of military style long gun assault rifles or other semi-automatic weapons.[49]

Under ATF supervision, straw purchasers bought large quantities of guns from Andre Howard's store. Many straw purchasers give off signs of nervousness; after all, they are committing a crime. But in Phoenix, the straw purchasers seemed confident, smiling, because they were flush with cash and had pulled this off so often without the slightest hitch.

The federal government's reassurances to the owners of shops like Lone Wolf, or J&G Sales in Prescott, or the Scottsdale Gun Club, did not totally ease gun shop owners' concerns. Several times throughout the operation, owners and their employees contacted the ATF, telling them they suspected weapons they were selling were not being put to recreational use or being bought for legitimate self-defense, but were destined for criminal activities. They cooperated with the ATF but wanted to make sure the ATF was planning on doing something before these guns were put to criminal use.[50]

As one ATF agent put it to me, there was an underlying sense of intimidation in ATF's activities with gun shop owners: "You see your license? We control whether you get approved for this license and therefore control whether or not you get to stay in business, keep earning a paycheck. Are you *really* going to say no to helping us with this operation?"[51]

Despite their assurances to gun shop owners and employees, the ATF did not have a reliable means for tracking the weaponry. On one occasion, Agent John Dodson went on his own to Radio Shack to buy supplies for homemade tracking devices with ATF funds. Dodson managed to build a GPS device and put it into an AK-47 variant rifle bought by a straw purchaser. The battery ran out within forty hours of leaving the store. Out of 2,500 guns sold during Fast and Furious, a total of two (including Dodson's) were attached to GPS devices. Once the guns were taken into Mexico, the ATF's authority and jurisdiction over them vanished, making tracing the guns to the source all but impossible.

"I can't think of a single, logical strategy as to why this would have worked," Special ATF Agent Peter Forcelli said.[52]

But perhaps it was not supposed to "work" all along.

CHAPTER FOUR

WHAT THE HELL ARE WE DOING?

"I was angry. I'm still angry. This is not what we do."

—Former ATF Attaché to Mexico Darren Gil

"We weren't giving guns to people who were hunting bear, we were giving guns to people who were killing other humans."

—ATF Special Agent Peter Forcelli

By late 2009, ATF agents stationed in Mexico, working blood-soaked crime scenes from Mexicali to Nogales to Obregon,[1] found a common denominator in the abandoned firearms littered around the corpses.[2] Each had near tamper-proof serial numbers that traced back to Phoenix-area gun stores.[3] Darren Gil, the ATF's former attaché to Mexico, remembers reporting to the Phoenix office—to Special Agent in Charge Bill Newell, his deputy George Gillett, and Group Supervisor of Phoenix Group VII David Voth—"Hey, we're getting an abnormal number of traces."[4] The response, as Gil described it, was, "We have an ongoing investigation. We have a ton of resources on it. Thanks for calling and making us aware. We'll follow up from here."

Gil found the response wholly unsatisfying. "It was inconceivable in my mind for any competent ATF Special Agent to allow firearms to disappear at all," he said.[5] "It [was] even more inconceivable that a competent ATF Special Agent would allow firearms to cross an international border, knowing that they are ultimately destined for the hands of the 'worst of the worst' criminals in the Western Hemisphere."[6]

Gil promptly contacted ATF's headquarters at the Justice Department in Washington, D.C. In a conversation with the ATF's chief of International Affairs, Gil was again assured there was an ongoing investigation with "cooperative" gun shops and that everything was "under control." "It sounded like a significant investigation," Gil said.[7] Gil didn't even find out about the name "Operation Fast and Furious" until December 2010.

■   ■   ■   ■   ■

On March 5, 2010, top ATF officials received a briefing from David Voth in Washington, D.C., focused solely on Fast and Furious. Among those attending were Newell (by video), the ATF's Deputy Director William Hoover, Bill McMahon, then deputy director for operations in the West, and Mark Chait, assistant director for field operations. ATF Special Agents in Charge were also in attendance by video conference. By the time of the spring meeting, more than 1,026 weapons had been successfully trafficked into Mexico through Fast and Furious; straw purchasers had spent $649,745.32 on ammunition and guns. The briefing included charts listing the names of straw purchasers, straw purchaser connections to each other, their relationship to the Sinaloa Cartel, how much money straw purchasers had spent, and the details of fifteen recoveries of weapons at crime scenes over a five-month period. This was an operation of remarkable scale by ATF standards: a typical operation involves twelve guns on average.[8]

Kenneth Melson, the acting director of the ATF and an Obama appointee, made a separate visit to Phoenix that March. Melson, a veteran federal prosecutor, received a briefing on Fast and Furious and requested the IP address for the live video feed monitoring straw purchasers in cooperating gun shops; he wanted to watch the transactions from his corner office at ATF headquarters. From this point forward, Melson received weekly briefings on the operation.[9]

One of Eric Holder's deputies at the Justice Department, Gary Grindler, also went to the ATF Phoenix Field Division. He too was briefed on the details of Fast and Furious. Among other things, Grindler was told about the most prolific straw purchaser, Uriel Patino, and how many guns he had purchased with ATF assistance. Grindler took notes, scribbling on a photocopied picture of guns that had been collected from violent crime scenes in Mexico.[10]

Eric Holder's assistant attorney general Lanny Breuer praised the Phoenix office for their good work on gun trafficking, saying their efforts would give the department a "big win."[11] Breuer signed off on Title-3 (T-3) wiretaps for the Fast and Furious program in spring 2010, allowing agents to listen to phone conversations of Uriel Patino, Jaime Avila, and other straw purchasers.

In order for T-3 wiretaps to be approved, agents or management officials have to provide specific details about why they need them and how they will be used to move a case forward. Wiretaps are used as a last resort. In addition, a United States attorney—in this case, Dennis Burke—has to recommend approval. The attorney general or his designated subordinate at the Justice Department then reviews the request, the criminal offense that is being monitored, the risks or dangers of the case, where and for how long wiretaps will be installed, names of the suspects being monitored, and other facts before granting approval.[12]

■ ■ ■ ■ ■

Within the ATF, the massive size of Operation Fast and Furious made it something of a conversation piece. Special Agent Peter Forcelli was working in the home invasions and violent crime division of the ATF when he heard other agents boast of an operation involving 1,200 firearms.

"My thought at the time is that they went and identified a group of individuals that were buying firearms and they went and pulled the records and that these people had purchased 1,200 guns and they were building a good case," Forcelli recalled.[13] But then things became more unusual. "They were talking about surveillance. They were talking about all kinds of things but they're not talking about interviewing anybody."

Forcelli was present at a meeting where Hope MacAllister gave a PowerPoint presentation with photographs of straw purchasers buying guns in Phoenix-area gun stores. Forcelli was left with the impression that videotapes of the transactions had been given to the ATF by gun shop owners who thought these gun buys were suspicious. He assumed arrests were imminent. He didn't know that all of the purchases had been allowed to occur by the ATF from the beginning and witnessed in real-time.

A colleague corrected Forcelli, "Dude, we were out there watching these take place."[14]

Privately, Forcelli asked George Gillett, the Phoenix office's deputy, about the questionable tactics being used. Gillett leaned back, put his hands behind his head, and said, "That isn't your concern."[15]

Forcelli asked his supervisor, Jim Needles, about the operation. Needles said, "If you or I were running the case, it wouldn't be getting run this way."

Whatever his misgivings, Forcelli was not directly involved in the operation. John Dodson, however, was, and he repeatedly expressed his doubts about "Fast and Furious" to his superiors in the Phoenix office. Management was not sympathetic.

"It has been brought to my attention that there may be a schism developing amongst the group," David Voth wrote in a March 12 email to all special agents in Group VII. He continued:

> We are all entitled to our respective (albeit different) opinions however we all need to get along and realize that we have a mission to accomplish....
>
> Whether you care or not people of rank and authority at HQ are paying close attention to this case and they also believe we (Phoenix Group VII) are doing what they envisioned the Southwest Border Groups doing. It may sound cheesy, but we are "The tip of the ATF spear" when it comes to Southwest Border Firearms Trafficking....

I will be damned if this case is going to suffer due to petty arguing, rumors or other adolescent behavior.

I don't know what all the issues are but we are all adults, we are all professionals, and we have a [*sic*] exciting opportunity to use the biggest tool in our law enforcement tool box. If you don't think this is fun you're in the wrong line of work—period! This is the pinnacle of domestic U.S. law enforcement techniques. After this the tool box is empty. Maybe the Maricopa County Jail is hiring detention officers and you can get paid $30,000 (instead of $100,000) to serve lunch to the inmates all day.[16]

In March 2010, as part of the "fun" of Operation Fast and Furious, the ATF allowed 359 high-powered weapons to be walked into Mexico. It was the most violent month in Mexico in five years.

■ ■ ■ ■ ■

Darren Gil was stunned that the ever-mounting number of Phoenix-sold guns at Mexican crime scenes came to cartel members courtesy of the United States government. He felt, he said, as if he was "in the eye of a perfect storm of idiocy."[17] He had not been informed about the operation beforehand and now he found himself being prevented from learning more. His phone calls to Washington went unanswered, and he was locked out of the ATF's tracing database. "We were entering the data but weren't getting the trace results back, all we were getting was 'trace information delayed,'" he later reported. "And what that generally means is, there's been a hold on it either by the tracing center or by a field division because they didn't want that information released for some particular reason."[18] His conclusion was that someone in Phoenix didn't want any more queries from Mexico.

Gil's questions grew increasingly pointed. "Hey, when are they going to shut this, to put it bluntly, damn investigation down?" he quotes himself as saying. "We're getting hurt down here."[19] Finally an answer came down from Washington. Gil was promised that the program would be shut down by July 2010. That turned out to be false.

On June 10, 2010, as complaints from ATF agents in Mexico escalated, Hope MacAllister asked the National Tracing Center to hold off on tracing guns that were being recovered in Mexico. The National Tracing Center waited for instructions on when to resume tracing the guns. They never received such orders. It appeared the Phoenix office did not want the Mexican government or ATF agents in Mexico to know that so many of the guns were traceable to gun shops cooperating with Fast and Furious.

To members of Group VII in Phoenix, David Voth was again expressing great progress. "Our subjects purchased 359 firearms during the month of March alone, to include numerous Barrett .50 caliber rifles," Voth said in an April 2 email. "I believe we are righteous in our plan to dismantle this entire organization and to rush in to arrest any one person without taking in to account the entire scope of the conspiracy would be ill advised to the overall good of the mission."[20]

Voth was aware that the stated objective of the program—reducing cross-border violence with Mexico—was a failure. In at least one email, Voth even noted the unfavorable statistics—842 people killed in December 2009, shortly after Fast and Furious began, 937 in January, 988 in February,[21] and 1,200 killed in March 2010—but seemed to make no connection to the program or to see that these figures might cast doubt on Fast and Furious being a "righteous"[22] success; indeed 2010 ended with 15,273 murders attributed to Mexican drug cartels, the highest number on record.

If Voth didn't see the connection, Dodson did and asked his supervisors about it.[23] He was told, in that horrible cliché, "If you are going to make an omelet, you need to scramble some eggs."[24] He didn't accept that answer. He repeatedly approached case agent Hope MacAllister and Supervisor David Voth with questions. What, Dodson asked, was the purpose of allowing guns to walk into Mexico? Didn't they understand that people were going to die? Dodson's fellow agents in Group VII were also having doubts. "On at least a couple of occasions that I witnessed, Special Agent Dodson asked both Special Agent MacAllister and Group Supervisor Voth if they were prepared to attend the funeral of a slain agent or officer after he or she was killed with one of those straw-purchased firearms. Neither one answered or even seemed concerned by the question posed to them," Special Agent Olindo Casa, who was also part of Group VII, said.[25]

Gun dealers tasked by the ATF with the sale of weapons to known cartel affiliates were also getting worried. On June 17, 2010, a concerned gun dealer emailed David Voth directly:

> As per our discussion about over communicating I wanted to share some concerns that came up. Tuesday night I watched a segment of a Fox News report about firearms and

the border. The segment, if the information was correct, is disturbing to me. When you, Emory and I met on May 13th I shared my concerns with you guys that I wanted to make sure that none of the firearms that were sold per our conversation with you and various ATF agents could or would ever end up south of the border or in the hands of the bad guys. I guess I am looking for a bit of reassurance that the guns arc not getting south or in wrong hands. I know it is an ongoing investigation so there is limited information you can share with me. But as I said in our meeting, I want to help ATF with its investigation but not at the risk of agents [*sic*] safety because I have some very close friends that are U.S. Border Patrol agents in southern AZ as well as my concern for all the agents [*sic*] safety that protect our country. If possible please email me back and share with me any reassurances that you can. As always thank you for your time and I send this email with all respect and a heart felt concern to do the right thing.[26]

Voth responded by thanking the dealer for contacting him about his concerns and offered to stop by his store to speak with him.[27] Reportedly Voth told the gun shop owner everything was fine: guns weren't being sent over the border and into Mexico.

On August 25, 2010, a full month after Darren Gil was told by Washington the operation would end, David Voth received an email from a cooperating gun shop that Patino had placed an order over the phone asking for twenty FN-FNX 9mm firearms. The gun shop only had four in stock, and wanted to know if Voth recommended they fulfill Patino's entire order. "I am requesting your guidance as to whether or not we should perform the transaction, as it is outside of the standard way we have been dealing with him."[28]

Voth advised the shop to order the weapons Patino requested.

Not only did Voth encourage gun shops to make illegal arms sales, but he and Hope MacAllister actually instructed gun shop owners like Andre Howard of Lone Wolf Trading Company on how to file their taxes in such a way that would prevent IRS inquiries, which otherwise might happen because of the spikes in their shops' incomes.[29]

■ ■ ■ ■ ■

In Washington, meanwhile, the Obama administration was making quiet efforts to pass more restrictive gun laws. President Obama's chief of staff Rahm Emanuel did not want administration gun control policies to be a problem for Democrats in midterm elections,[30] but President Obama assured Second Amendment opponent Sarah Brady of the Brady Campaign to Prevent Gun Violence that his administration was working on gun control measures "under the radar."[31]

On July 14, 2010, the ATF's Washington-based Assistant Director in Charge of Field Operations, Mark Chait, sent an email to Bill Newell. "Can you see if these guns were all purchased from the same FFL [Federal Firearm Licensee, or gun shop] and at one time. We are looking at anecdotal cases to support a demand letter on long gun [guns with long barrels, such as rifles and shotguns, as opposed to handguns] multiple sales."[32] In other words, Chait was attempting to use the guns sold by cooperating gun shops that were part of Fast and

Furious as evidence for a "demand letter" supporting new gun control regulations. Deputy Attorney General Gary Grindler's handwritten notes from the March 2010 meeting in Phoenix suggested a similar intent.[33] Next to a photo of long gun rifles recovered in Mexico— weapons he knew were part of the Fast and Furious operation—he scrawled "no long reporting measure."

In autumn 2010, ATF Director Ken Melson pushed Congress for a long gun reporting measure for multiple sales of rifles in border state gun shops. At the same time, Mayors Against Illegal Guns issued a report dedicated to blaming U.S. gun shops for Mexican drug cartel violence, a group Obama Chief of Staff Rahm Emanuel would join after leaving the White House to become Chicago's mayor in 2011.[34]

■　■　■　■　■

By October 2010, the Phoenix evidence vault was brimming with guns recovered at crime scenes in Mexico, many of which had been used in murders.

Frustrated at the run-around he had been given by the bureau, Darren Gil retired in December 2010. His replacement as ATF attaché to Mexico, Carlos Canino, asked his superiors for permission to inform Mexican authorities about Operation Fast and Furious and its connection to the recent spate of murders.

Then, on December 15, 2010, came an occurrence that would change everything. An alert was issued to the U.S. Attorney's Office, Border Patrol, ATF, and multiple local law enforcement agencies: shots had been fired near Nogales, Arizona; an agent was down.

With Border Patrol and FBI agents on the scene, the abandoned guns used by the rip crew that had attacked Terry and his fellow agents were seized as evidence and labeled by the FBI for further inquiry.

By the early morning hours of Wednesday, December 15, 2010, Josephine Terry knew her son had been killed. John Dodson's nightmare of a U.S. law enforcement officer killed with an AK-47 that the ATF had let walk to Mexico had come true.

The guns used to kill Brian Terry were purchased by Jaime Avila on January 16, 2010. On that occasion, Avila had purchased fifty-two firearms, including FN 5.7 pistols, a Barrett 50 BMG rifle, AK-47 variant rifles, Ruger 9mm handguns, and a Colt .38 super. He paid for the entire arsenal in cash.[35]

"My heart sank, I couldn't breathe," ATF Special Agent and whistleblower Vince Cefalu said, describing his reaction when he learned of Terry's death.[36]

"I felt guilty," Dodson later reflected. "I mean it's crushing. I don't know how to explain it."[37]

He was not alone. Explaining Fast and Furious would turn out to be a major problem.

CHAPTER FIVE

PANIC

"I don't like the perception that we allowed guns to 'walk.'"

—Bill Newell, ATF Phoenix Director

wo hundred miles away in Phoenix, Dennis Burke was spending a late night catching up on his emails. At 2:14 in the morning, just minutes before learning that a Border Patrol agent had been shot, Burke sent an email to Monty Wilkinson, Eric Holder's longtime friend and deputy chief of staff. "We have a major gun trafficking case connected to Mexico we are taking down in January. 20+ defendants. Will call today to explain in detail."[1]

An hour and fifteen minutes later, Burke's staff members forwarded a message from Marco Lopez, chief of staff for U.S. Customs and Border Protection.

"Agent has passed away," the message said.

"Thx," Burke replied by email. "Horrible." He turned in to get some sleep. It would be a long day in the U.S. Attorney's Office.

■ ■ ■ ■ ■

Local newspapers and broadcast stations reported on Brian Terry's death before the Border Patrol issued its official press release. KVOA News 4 in Tucson reported, "U.S. Border Patrol agents are still searching for a fifth suspect in the killing of agent Brian Terry. Three suspects are in custody, and one is in the hospital for surgery, following the shooting and killing of the agent late Tuesday night."[2] A *Nogales International* headline read, "Authorities hunt for suspect in Border Patrol agent's killing."[3] Nationally, his death was reported by Fox News and CNN.

The morning after Terry's death, Holder's deputy chief of staff Monty Wilkinson wrote to Burke at 10:04 a.m., "Tragic, I've alerted the AG, the Acting DAG, Lisa, etc." Attorney General Eric Holder had been directly informed of Brian's death.[4]

That afternoon, Dennis Burke learned that the guns were traced to the operation he and Assistant U.S. Attorney Emory Hurley had green-lighted. He immediately called Newell at the Phoenix ATF. At 5:19 p.m. Burke wrote to his staff mentioning two of the guns seized at Brian's murder scene were connected to an ongoing investigation out of the ATF Phoenix Field Office.

"The guns tie back to Emory's Fast and Furious case," Burke wrote in an email to Acting Arizona U.S. Attorney Ann Scheel at 7:24 p.m. on December 15, 2011.[5]

Burke also emailed Wilkinson with an update on the details: "The guns found near the murder[ed] BP officer connect back to the investigation we were going to talk about—they were AK-47s purchased at a Phoenix gun store."

Wilkinson responded with, "I'll call tomorrow." It was late on the East Coast.

A joint press conference held by the Border Patrol, the FBI, and the U.S. Attorney's Office had taken place earlier the same day, at 5:00 p.m. Burke was reluctant to hold a press conference. Matt Chandler, Janet Napolitano's deputy press secretary, urged the U.S. attorney to go on the offense and express outrage over the murder of a Border Patrol officer. He suggested Burke send someone to the press event who would "vow to prosecute [straw purchasers] to the full extent."[6]

Officials from Homeland Security, ATF, and the U.S. attorney's office worked together to hone their message to the media. The press briefing was short, less than five minutes long. Neither Dennis Burke nor Emory Hurley showed up. They instead sent second-tier staffers from the U.S. Attorney's Office to look on.

Border Patrol Deputy Chief Richard Barlow took the podium first. His remarks were brief and solemn. He explained that Brian Terry had been shot and killed in the line of duty as he encountered suspects near Rio Rico, Arizona. Suspects had been taken into custody. He commended Terry, saying his fellow agents had the utmost respect for him, and then said, "This is a stark reminder of the realities we face each and every day in protecting this border and protecting our communities. There are people that wake up every day with nothing else on their mind but to do harm on the citizens of this country and our way of life." Barlow added, "This is an ongoing investigation so there won't be any of the particulars discussed with the incident."[7]

At the ATF's Phoenix Field Office, the news of Brian Terry's death spread quickly. When John Dodson learned of the news, he was horrified. His prophecy that the operation he was tasked with implementing would end up facilitating the murder of his fellow law enforcement officers had come true.

Jaime Avila had been under surveillance for over a year. He had purchased hundreds of high-powered weapons, but it was not until Brian Terry's death that he was arrested—within twenty-four hours of the killing. There was no shortage of evidence implicating him as an illegal weapons purchaser, but ATF's Phoenix field office management—Bill Newell, George Gillett, David Voth, and Hope MacAllister—were playing damage control with frantic meetings, phone calls, and emails.[8] Newell and Voth ignored the mass of evidence that linked Avila to the Fast and Furious program and instead sought to minimize their exposure.

At 11:41 p.m.—almost twenty-four hours after Terry was killed—David Voth sent an email to Newell, Gillett, and ATF Phoenix office supervisor Jim Needles. "We are charging Avila with a standalone June 2010 firearms purchase where he used a bad (old) address on the 4473 [924(a)(1)(A)—false records required to be kept by dealer]. This way we do not divulge our current case (Fast and Furious) or the Border Patrol Shooting Case."

Voth and his colleagues Newell, Gillett, and MacAllister wanted to keep Fast and Furious secret, but the dozens of ATF agents who knew about Fast and Furious and had lodged complaints about it long before Terry's death made that impossible. One ATF supervisor in the El Paso office familiar with Phoenix's gunwalking tactics wrote an email to his assistant special agent in charge: "Maybe Phoenix should start preparing their explanation for the way that they conducted their straw purchase cases there. They should probably hire a media expert anyway to assist them in explaining the 2,000 firearms and the possible connection in the murder of the Border Patrol Agent."[9]

In the wake of the Terry murder, Fast and Furious had to be shut down. Burke and Newell scrambled to assemble indictments of the straw purchasers Fast and Furious had followed. At the same time they were careful to downplay the scope of the arms sales they had sanctioned. Bill Newell didn't want it said that his ATF office had allowed guns to "walk," even though that is exactly what happened. There was no direct link between Fast and Furious and Terry's death, he insisted. In an email to a colleague, Newell wrote,

> For what it's worth and since I don't like the perception that we allowed guns to "walk," I had David Voth pull the numbers of the guns recovered in Mexico as well as those we had a direct role in taking off here in the US. Almost all of the 350 seized in the US were done based on our info and in such a way to not burn the wire or compromise the bigger case. The guns purchased early on in the case we couldn't have stopped mainly because we weren't fully aware of all the players at that time and people buying multiple firearms in Arizona is a very common thing.[10]

The news worked its way through the Justice Department. On December 17, Acting Deputy Attorney General, Gary Grindler who had known about the details of Fast and Furious since March 2010, received an email from another Department of Justice official.

"You may recall that a CBP [Customs and Border Patrol] border agent was killed on Tuesday in a firefight in Arizona along the Mexican border. Two of the weapons recovered from the scene (AK-47 variants) have been linked to Jaime Avila Jr. a straw firearms purchaser that ATF and USAO [U.S. Attorney's Office] for Arizona have been investigating since November 2009 as part of its larger Fast and Furious operation."[11]

Dennis Burke flew to Michigan to visit Josephine Terry. "He was just trying to explain to us exactly what happened in a roundabout way, we really never got anything out of the visit that he did have," she said.[12] Burke did not reveal that the guns found at her son's murder scene were connected to a government program; Josephine Terry learned that later, from the media.

Homeland Security Secretary Janet Napolitano sent her condolences to Brian's family. "The fatal shooting of Border Patrol Agent Brian A. Terry last night is an unconscionable act of violence against the men and women of the Border Patrol and all those who serve and defend our country," Napolitano said. "We will honor his memory by remaining resolute and committed to the serious task of securing our nation's borders. I ask that all of us keep Agent Terry and his family in our prayers."[13]

She attended Brian's funeral, offering a speech in tribute to the fallen officer. "He put service before self, which is the mark of heroism," Napolitano said during the service in front of hundreds of people. "I'm also proud to be carrying a personal note to you from the President of the United States to your family. He, like I, honors border patrol agent Brian Terry."[14]

If the words were meant to comfort the Terry family, they were found lacking. The family thought Napolitano's words were hollow and empty. "Now she can get on the news and say how she called the family of agent Brian Terry," Brian's stepmother told a local news reporter. "We didn't get one answer from her. She talked around everything just like the president does."[15]

Brian's father, Kent Terry, hoped his son didn't die "for nothing," and that the U.S. government would shut down illegal activity on the border. Napolitano responded to Terry's death by ordering more Border Patrol agents to monitor the area where he had been killed.

■ ■ ■ ■ ■

On January 8, 2011, two weeks after the Terry family buried their son, Congresswoman Gabrielle Giffords held a meet and greet event with constituents at a Safeway parking lot in Tucson. The event was meant to kick off a "Congress on Your Corner" series in congressional districts across the United States. Affable, energetic, and one of the few remaining centrist Democrats in the House of Representatives, Giffords was well liked by her colleagues, including conservative Republicans.

As the event began, a deranged young man approached the table where Giffords was visiting with constituents. At point blank range, he shot her with a 9mm handgun. The bullet went into the side of her head and through her brain. He then turned to the crowd and started shooting indiscriminately. The gunman ran out of bullets and reached for a second clip of ammunition when Patricia Maisch tackled him, preventing him from killing anybody else.

In total, the troubled Jared Loughner killed six people and severely wounded fourteen others. Among the murdered were U.S. District Court Judge John Roll and nine-year-old Christina Green.

Loughner was a high school dropout. His classmates described him as "sketchy,"[16] possibly dangerous, and someone whose political ideas were neither left nor right, nor well-informed.[17] He had a YouTube page filled with bizarre videos and rambling rants. He believed in conspiracy theories—including that the United States government was engaging in mind control and was behind the September 11 terrorist attacks—and sought to make his own currency to, in his words, "control the world." He had been kicked out of Pima Community College for strange behavior and for making threats against students and teachers. He was told that to be able to re-enroll, he would have to undergo a mental health evaluation. He had a history of drug use.

Loughner had an inexplicable obsession with Giffords, dating back to 2007 when he asked her a question at a town hall meeting: "What is government if words have no meaning?" Loughner saved a form letter her office sent as a thank you for attending the event. He kept it in a box, inside an envelope with the words "die bitch" and "assassination plans have been made" inscribed on it. Before the shooting, multiple complaints about Loughner's behavior had been reported to the Pima County Sheriff's Office and were ignored.[18] Watching news accounts of the Giffords shooting, ATF agents who had been nauseated by the murder of Brian Terry felt that same ache in the pits of their stomachs. "Please don't let this be one of our guns," they prayed.[19] As it turned out, Loughner had acquired his gun on November 30, 2010, at a Sportsman's Warehouse in Tucson, where Operation Fast and Furious was not being conducted.

Federal officials responded to the Giffords shooting in predictable fashion: by insisting that gun control laws be strengthened, that the

Clinton assault weapons ban be reinstated, and that high-capacity magazines like the one used by Loughner be banned. For the moment, the story of the shooting of a congresswoman and her heroic recovery diverted attention from the looming scandal of Fast and Furious. But it wouldn't last long.

■　■　■　■　■

It wasn't the mainstream media that uncovered the truth about Fast and Furious—it was a handful of bloggers and whistleblowers. Fast and Furious was first exposed to the public at CleanUpATF.org. The website had been founded in 2009 as an online forum for agents to expose wrongdoing in the bureau. Shortly after Brian Terry's death, anonymous users on the site suggested that there was an ATF program that deliberately trafficked guns across the border into Mexico.

"Mexican authorities were kept in the dark, and protests that they should be informed were overridden, first by the Phoenix ATF office, and ultimately by higher-ups in Washington, DC," one post said.[20] Another, "A gun used in this operation was involved in a December 2010 incident in which a Border Patrol agent was killed."[21]

Commenters on the site were outraged. "Can you believe ATF let guns walk into Mexico?" was a question that was asked in disbelief, repeatedly. "ATF management was allowing potentially hundreds of semiautomatic firearms to be walked across the Mexican border in order to pad statistics used to further budget and power objectives."

The chatter immediately gained the attention of two bloggers, Mike Vanderboegh and David Codrea. Working together, they vetted the information through their vast network of informants in the ATF.

They confirmed that Fast and Furious was a real operation, and guns, willfully passed to cartel associates by the ATF, had felled a federal law enforcement agent. Vanderboegh reached out to sources through an anonymous email system called the "Desert Telegraph" and connected them with the staff of Senator Charles Grassley, the seventy-seven-year-old Iowan who was the ranking Republican on the Senate Judiciary Committee. David Codrea, who edits two popular Second Amendment blogs and writes for the Examiner.com, noted that he and Vanderboegh "were both contacted independently by various ATF insiders claiming to have corroborating information and documentation." Codrea was careful to protect his sources' identities so they would not face retaliation from the Department of Justice or the ATF.

■ ■ ■ ■ ■

When Newell announced his gun trafficking indictments at a press conference on January 25, 2011, the information on Fast and Furious was only beginning to leak. Under the law covering gun trafficking, straw purchasers can be charged with a slew of offenses: smuggling goods from the United States, dealing firearms without a license, transferring firearms to a non-resident of the state, making a false statement in connection to the acquisition of a firearm, international firearms trafficking, use of a firearm in furtherance of a drug trafficking offense, conspiracy to commit any offense against the United States, and the attempt to export munitions without a license and evading reporting requirements. But Newell and the Arizona U.S. Attorney's office decided to settle on minor indictments, similar to Avila's indictment for putting knowingly false information on an ATF

4473 Form. At the same time, Newell asserted that the arrest of low level straw purchasers somehow amounted to a major takedown of the drug cartels.[22] Avila was charged with filling out an ATF 4473 Form with knowingly false information. With what would later be seen as galling hypocrisy, Newell proclaimed that straw purchasers like Avila "have as much blood on their hands as the criminals that use them."[23]

Newell claimed the indictments constituted a major takedown of the Mexican cartels. "We strongly believe we took down the entire organization from top to bottom that operated out of the Phoenix area," he said. He failed to make clear, however, that the suspects being charged were low level straw purchasers, not major cartel leaders.

Arizona U.S. Attorney Dennis Burke, also at the press conference, said his office was committed to stopping the illegal flow of guns into Mexico, and added that "the massive size of this operation exemplified the magnitude of the problem. Mexican Drug Lords go shopping for war weapons in Arizona."[24] He did not mention that the gun shops that had sold these guns would not have done so had it not been on orders from the ATF.

Reporter Dennis Wagner of the *Arizona Republic* asked Newell whether the ATF ever allowed guns to "walk."

"Hell, no!" Newell replied.

The evidence would soon point to a different answer.

CHAPTER SIX

WELCOME TO MURDERGATE

"Those people are now being killed wholesale."
—ATF Special Agent Vince Cefalu

David Codrea and Mike Vanderboegh contacted the offices of three prominent U.S. senators known for their defense of the Second Amendment: Alabama's Jeff Sessions, Iowa's Charles Grassley, and Georgia's Saxby Chambliss, all Republicans. The senators' staffers, however, couldn't believe that a federal agency charged with stopping illegal trafficking would facilitate it.

If Capitol Hill staffers were inclined to ignore the charges, Justice Department officials knew better. Their own agents were leaking the details of the connection between Fast and Furious and the murder of Brian Terry, and it was only a matter of time before the story moved from the blogs of Codrea and Vanderboegh to the mainstream media.

A flood of IP addresses visiting CleanUpATF.org were linked back to Department of Justice computers.[1]

Thanks to Codrea's and Vanderboegh's relentless reporting, news of the scandal spread, and congressional offices that had ignored the bloggers before now had to deal with phone calls and emails from constituents who wanted answers. Senator Grassley's office took a particular interest in the issue, and when John Dodson stepped forward to talk about Fast and Furious, it was with Senator Grassley. Grassley was the top Republican on the Senate Judiciary Committee, which allowed him to dig into Fast and Furious and into the role the Justice Department played in the lethal operation.

Dodson risked his career by giving closed door testimony to Grassley and his staff. He revealed the bloody details of Fast and Furious, how it was carried out, who was giving orders, and how he had been instructed to facilitate the sale of weapons to the very cartels ATF claimed to be fighting. Grassley told Dodson that because he had identified potential wrongdoing by his ATF colleagues and superiors, he would be granted whistleblower protection so the ATF could not punish him.

Dodson dutifully reported to his superiors in Phoenix about his testimony to Senator Grassley. Dodson says that Newell and Gillett called him into a private office and ordered him to write a memo repudiating his testimony. Dodson refused.[2]

With Dodson's testimony, the methodical Senator Grassley believed he finally had enough probable cause to question Acting ATF Director Kenneth Melson and the Justice Department about gunwalking tactics used in the Phoenix Office. In a letter to the ATF dated January 27, 2011, Grassley stated: "Members of the Judiciary Committee have received numerous allegations that the ATF sanctioned the sale of hundreds of assault weapons to suspected straw purchasers, who then allegedly transported these weapons throughout the southwestern border area and into Mexico. These extremely serious allegations were accompanied by detailed documentation which appears to lend credibility to the claims and partially corroborates them."[3]

Grassley also asked Melson for a briefing on Project Gunrunner. When no response came, Grassley sent another letter to Melson. This time the tone was tougher.

"It appears that the ATF is reacting in less productive ways to my request," Grassley wrote in his January 31 letter. "As you may be aware, obstructing a Congressional investigation is a crime. Additionally, denying or interfering with employees' rights to furnish information to Congress is also against the law. Federal officials who deny or interfere with employees' rights to furnish information to Congress are not entitled to have their salaries paid by taxpayers' dollars."[4]

Officials at ATF and the Arizona U.S. Attorney's office did not appreciate Grassley's persistence. Dennis Burke emailed Deputy Assistant Attorney General Jason Weinstein in Washington, D.C. Weinstein worked closely with Deputy Attorney General Lanny Breuer.[5] "Grassley's assertions regarding the Arizona investigation and the weapons recovered at the BP Agent scene are based on categorical falsehoods. I worry that ATF will take 8 months to answer this when they should be refuting its underlying accusations right now," Burke wrote.[6]

Eric Holder's deputy Lanny Breuer reassured ATF Acting Director Melson that the Department of Justice supported ATF in an email. "On Gunrunner. Ken. We support ATF 100 percent."[7]

Breuer approved a response to Grassley, after carefully reviewing every word. The letter, sent to Grassley on February 4, 2011, was signed by Assistant Attorney General Ronald Weich.[8]

"At the outset, the allegation described in your January 27 letter—that ATF 'sanctioned' or otherwise knowingly allowed the sale of assault weapons to straw purchasers who then transported them to Mexico—is false," Weich wrote. Weich agreed to give Grassley the briefing he requested, but said it would not address the "on-going criminal investigation" of Project Gunrunner, the first of many times the Obama administration would cite an "on-going investigation" as an excuse not to submit information to Congress.

Weich wrote, "As you know, the Department has a long-standing policy against the disclosure of non-public information about pending criminal investigations, which protects the independence and effectiveness of our law enforcement efforts as well as the privacy and due process interests of individuals who may or may not ever be charged with criminal offenses."

Grassley had not asked for a public briefing. Nonetheless the Obama Justice Department had laid down a marker: it would be unwilling to cooperate. Grassley staffers knew that to get more information, they had to turn up the heat. They encouraged John Dodson to go public.

■ ■ ■ ■ ■

On February 15, 2011, 32-year-old Special Immigration and Customs Enforcement Agent Jaime Zapata and his partner, Victor Avila, were driving their blue Chevy Suburban SUV on a busy, four-lane

Mexican highway. They were headed back to the United States after a meeting at the U.S. Embassy in Mexico City. Though their vehicle was armored and had diplomatic license plates, Zapata and Avila weren't personally armed, following Mexican law that prohibits U.S. agents working in Mexico from carrying weapons.

It is believed that two SUVs pulled up alongside them, the drivers gesturing for Avila and Zapata to pull over. This was not something U.S. agents wanted to do on a Mexican highway.

After a brief car chase, the Americans' SUV was forced off the road. Their vehicle disabled, they cracked open the passenger side window to speak with a man approaching them. The man was armed with an AK-47 variant rifle. Even as Zapata and Avila identified themselves as U.S. diplomats, the man placed the barrel of his gun into the cabin and unleashed a barrage of bullets. Zapata was killed instantaneously; Avila was severely injured with gunshot wounds to his legs.[9]

Two days later, the Associated Press quoted Texas Congressman Michael McCaul as saying the U.S. Federal Agents had been targeted by the Zeta drug gang:

> "This was a complete ambush," Texas Rep. Michael McCaul said, adding that investigators recovered at least 90 bullet casings from the scene.
>
> The Texas Republican said Zapata and Avila identified themselves as U.S. diplomats "hoping they (the Zetas) would honor the long-standing tradition that they don't (target) U.S. law enforcement."
>
> "This is a complete game changer," he said. "They are changing the rules."

He said while the motive for the attack remains unclear, one
thing is certain: "There's no case of mistaken identity."[10]

Washington reacted swiftly. From the Justice Department, Attorney
General Holder announced the creation of a task force with the
Department of Homeland Security and FBI to investigate the shooting.

"The murder of Special Agent Jaime Zapata and the shooting of
another ICE agent provide a sad reminder of the dangers American
law enforcement officers face every day," Holder stated in a release.
"Working with our Mexican counterparts, we have already launched
an aggressive investigation, and this joint task force will ensure that
every available resource is used to bring the perpetrators of this terrible crime to justice."[11]

Janet Napolitano, who had now lost two agents two months apart
due to Mexican cartel violence, also praised the new joint task force as
a reflection of "our commitment to bring the investigatory and
prosecutorial power of the U.S. government to bear as we work with
the Mexican government to bring these criminals to justice."[12]

It was not long before rumors circulated that the AK-47 used in
the shooting was linked to Fast and Furious. A Dallas area man, Otilio
Osorio, who had been under ATF surveillance for months, was accused
of buying the guns used in Zapata's murder and arrested for gun
smuggling.

Even worse for the ATF, suspicion arose that the gunwalking techniques employed in the Phoenix field office's Operation Fast and
Furious were being replicated elsewhere. Reports surfaced that
Carter's Country Gun Store, located in Houston, had sold weapons
to straw purchasers at the request of the ATF. Houston Defense Attor-

ney Dick DeGuerin explained on the NRA News Radio program *Cam & Company*:

> **DeGuerin:** "Carter's Country was doing what the ATF had asked them to do and that was to go through with sales that sometimes they may not have made on their own. They might have said, 'Well, this looks a little suspicious.' But the ATF agents that were dealing with…the personnel at Carter's Country said, 'No, we need your help. We want to follow these guns. We want to know who the people are and you can help us.' So that's what Carter's Country did. They tried to be the good citizens that they were asked to be, and have always been, only to have it blow up in their face."

> **Edwards:** "And as you say, they said they were going to follow these guns; and as we know, some of them ended up in Mexico, which sounds an awful lot like Operation Fast and Furious."[13]

"I've heard Carter's Country's reports of how things were working and it sounds identical," an insider source who requested anonymity told me.[14]

The Department of Justice's task force assembled by Holder has refused to confirm or deny any links between Zapata's death and Fast and Furious.

"The likelihood that these were Fast and Furious guns is certainly plausible," said the family's attorney. "What happened with Jaime needs to come out."[15]

Mary Zapata, Jaime's mother, has expressed fears of a government cover-up.[16] The Zapata family has had to file Freedom of Information Act (FOIA) requests just to get minor details about their son's death. Like the Terry family, they have received no answers.

There were now two dead men linked to the Fast and Furious operation. There soon would be hundreds more.

■ ■ ■ ■ ■

The mainstream press finally woke up to the Fast and Furious story on February 23, 2011. CBS *Evening News* aired a story by Sharyl Attkisson, boasting exclusive anonymous sources who revealed the details of the Fast and Furious operation. Attkisson has garnered enemies in both political parties. She won an Emmy Award in 2009 for her investigations into the Bush administration's TARP bailout of Wall Street banks. In 2010 she was nominated for an Emmy for her reporting on Congress's frivolous pork barrel spending. Through her reporting, CBS became one of the few mainstream media sources to break any part of the Fast and Furious story.

Attkisson commented that the Fast and Furious scandal was "so large, some insiders say it surpasses the shoot-out at Ruby Ridge and the deadly siege at Waco." Sources told her flat out that the ATF "facilitated the delivery of thousands of guns into criminal hands." Aside from six whistleblowers who chose to remain anonymous, fearing retribution, no one at ATF headquarters would talk to her. Sources told her that gun shops involved in Fast and Furious had wanted "to stop the questionable sales, but ATF encouraged them to continue."

According to Attkisson, "One agent called the strategy 'insane.' Another said: 'We were fully aware the guns would probably be moved across the border to drug cartels where they could be used to kill.'" At least eleven agents, she reported, "expressed fierce opposition to the strategy," and warned that the guns would be used in crimes, which they soon were, including the shooting death of agent Brian Terry. It was alleged that more than 2,500 guns had been permitted to walk to the Mexican drug cartels, yet, "in a letter, the Justice Department which oversees ATF says the agency has never knowingly allowed the sale of assault weapons to suspected gunrunners."[17]

One week later, Attkisson featured an interview with John Dodson, who gave his first public account of the operation. "You were intentionally letting guns go to Mexico?" Attkisson asked him on camera.

"Yes ma'am," Dodson replied. "The agency was." Dodson became emotional. "I'm boots on the ground in Phoenix, telling you we've been doing it every day since I've been here," he said. "Here I am. Tell me I didn't do the things that I did. Tell me you didn't order me to do the things I did. Tell me it didn't happen. Now you have a name on it. You have a face to put with it. Here I am. Someone now, tell me it didn't happen."

When asked if he wanted to convey a message to the Terry family, Dodson's eyes looked wet with tears. "First of all, I'd tell them that I'm sorry. Second of all, I'd tell them I've done everything that I can for them to get the truth. After this, I don't know what else I can do. But I hope they get it."

After months of her digging, the Obama administration decided to express its displeasure with Attkisson's reporting.

The Justice Department's communications director Tracy Schmaler yelled at her over the phone. A White House spokesman, Eric Schultz, reportedly directed a barrage of expletives toward her.[18] As Attkisson explained, "The White House and Justice Department will tell you that I'm the only reporter—as they told me—that is not reasonable. They say the *Washington Post* is reasonable, the *LA Times* is reasonable, the *New York Times* is reasonable, I'm the only one who thinks this is a story, and they think I'm unfair and biased by pursuing it."[19]

The *New York Times* and *Washington Post* weren't just "reasonable," they seemed to act as press officers for the Obama administration. In one *New York Times* article, "Under Partisan Fire Eric Holder Soldiers On," reporter Charlie Savage did his best to portray Republican efforts to investigate the Fast and Furious scandal as a partisan witch hunt. "As Mr. Holder's third year as attorney general draws to a close, no member of President Obama's cabinet has drawn more partisan criticism," Savage wrote. "Mr. Holder contended that many of his other critics—not only elected Republicans but also a broader universe of conservative commentators and bloggers—were instead playing 'Washington gotcha' games, portraying them as frequently 'conflating things, conveniently leaving some stuff out, construing things to make it seem not quite what it was' to paint him and other department figures in the worst possible light."[20]

In June 2011, the *Washington Post* published an editorial defending the ATF against the "paranoia" of the NRA and the "gun rights lobby," accusing the Second Amendment defenders of fighting "against virtually every proposal to empower the bureau to better track and crack down on illegal firearms.... And they continue to fight new rules that would allow the bureau to track bulk sales of long guns that have played a major role in the drug-fueled violence in Mexico."[21]

Even before Fast and Furious broke on December 15, 2010, coincidentally the same day as Brian Terry's murder, the *Washington Post* attacked law-abiding gun shop owners along the border who, according to sources in the ATF and Justice Department, had no scruples about selling to straw purchasers. "A year-long investigation by the *Washington Post* has cracked that secrecy and uncovered the names of the top 12 U.S. dealers of guns traced to Mexico in the past two years."[22]

The article unwittingly stumbled on this truth: "What is different now, authorities say, is the number of high-powered rifles heading south—AR-15s, AK-47s, armor-piercing .50-caliber weapons—and the savagery of the violence." The *Post* neglected to report that "authorities" were green-lighting the sales of the very same "high-powered rifles" by the thousands to known cartel members. The *Post* story referred to Project Gunrunner as an operation to inspect, interdict, and seize guns from straw purchasers. It did not mention an ATF operation to *allow* straw purchasers to buy guns for the Mexican drug cartels. Some of the very same ATF and Justice Department officials who blamed American gun shops for the spike in Mexican gun crime had in fact been helping the drug cartels to help themselves to weapons for over a year.

"If you're a gun dealer and you see a 21- or 22-year-old young lady walk in and plop down $15,000 in cash to buy 20 AK-47s, you might want to ask yourself what she needs them for," Bill Newell told the *Post.* "If she says, 'Christmas presents,' technically the dealer doesn't have to ask for more."[23]

The ATF also leaked skewed eTrace data to the *Post* that showed a high volume of guns in Mexico coming from Lone Wolf Trading Company and J&G Sales. The *Post* did not report that the numbers were so high because these dealers cooperated with the ATF in Operation Fast and Furious.

To the extent *Washington Post* journalists covered the Fast and Furious story, it was to blame gun shops for knowingly selling arms to cartel members.[24]

Like the *New York Times* and the *Washington Post*, the explicitly liberal media treated the Fast and Furious story as the leftist magazine *Mother Jones* did, calling it "one of the right's latest conspiracy theories."[25] The left-wing news blog Talking Points Memo called the connection between Fast and Furious and the Obama administration's gun control agenda "outlandish."[26] *The Daily Show*'s Jon Stewart called it "f*****g crazy." MSNBC's Rachel Maddow said the coverage of Fast and Furious was a result of "the insane paranoid message from the NRA." The George Soros-funded Media Matters for America called it "hysterical rhetoric."[27] Chris Matthews said that those who deemed Fast and Furious worthy of investigation were "another strain of the crazy far right."[28]

■ ■ ■ ■ ■

Senator Grassley, however, was hardly a member of "the crazy far right." He was respected by Republicans and Democrats as an elder statesman. He had run afoul of Tea Party conservatives by voting for the 2008 Wall Street bailout. On March 9, 2011, Janet Napolitano appeared before the Senate Judiciary Committee and was briefly questioned under oath about Fast and Furious by Senator Grassley. She claimed she had only learned about Fast and Furious after Brian Terry was killed, stressing that her agency had no involvement in the operation with the ATF or the Department of Justice.

> **Grassley:** Did you ever discuss with anyone anything similar to the strategy described by whistleblowers in this case that of allowing guns to walk to make a bigger case against the cartels and if so I'd like an explanation.

> **Napolitano:** Uh, no, I was not so informed, uh, and I know however the attorney general has asked his inspector general to look at the operation.

> **Grassley:** I'd like to ask you how you feel about the fact that another agency's decision to put hundreds of guns into the hands of criminals on both sides of the border may have contributed to the death of Border Patrol Agent Brian Terry.

> **Napolitano:** Well, Senator Grassley, to date I have asked that question. My understanding is that the whole Terry matter is under investigation including the source of the guns that were held so I think it would be premature and inappropriate for me to comment on that right now.

Given that two of Napolitano's federal agents—Brian Terry and Jaime Zapata—were gunned down by Mexican drug cartels armed with weapons traceable to Operation Fast and Furious, it seems highly unlikely that she hadn't talked to Attorney General Eric Holder about it.

If Napolitano didn't know about Fast and Furious before the death of Brian Terry or Jaime Zapata, someone at the Department of Homeland Security did. "For every report written in ATF for Fast and Furious, a shadow report was written for ICE [Homeland Security's Immigration and Customs Enforcement]," a source told me, adding that the Department of Homeland Security received weekly Southwest Border Initiative briefings.[29]

In fact, ICE agent Lane France was assigned specifically as a co-case agent to ATF Gun Running Group VII, the same group John Dodson was in. France was on the same level of authority as ATF Agent Hope MacAllister and her supervisor David Voth. A Department of Justice and Department of Homeland Security fact sheet dated June 30, 2009, shows an agreement between ATF and ICE to "work together on investigations of international firearms trafficking and possession of firearms by illegal aliens." It said, "Both agencies are committed to working together to reduce firearms-related violence along the U.S. border."

Napolitano testified before the Senate Judiciary Committee that she was "not aware" of the ICE agent assigned to Fast and Furious but that she had become "aware of the ATF operation generally" since "the murders of Agent Terry and Agent Zapata."

On March 23, 2011, President Obama offered his first public response to the unfolding scandal. Univision's Jorge Ramos asked Obama, in a one-on-one interview, if he authorized Fast and Furious and asked whether Mexican President Felipe Calderon was properly informed of the operation.

"There have been problems," he told the reporter. "I heard on the news about this story—Fast and Furious—where, allegedly, guns were run into Mexico."

"First of all, I did not authorize it," the president responded when pressed further. "Eric Holder, the Attorney General, did not authorize it. He's been very clear that our policy is to catch gunrunners and put them into jail. So what he's done is he's assigned an inspector general to investigate exactly what happened."[30]

Each department of the federal government has its own inspector general that functions as an internal, supposedly independent ombudsman. In the Obama administration's case, the acting inspector general tasked with investigating Fast and Furious was Cynthia Schnedar. There was ample reason to question her independence. Schnedar worked closely with Eric Holder between 1994 and 1997 in the Clinton Justice Department. As an assistant U.S. attorney in Washington, D.C, she had reported to Holder who was then U.S. attorney for Washington. They worked on numerous cases together, including cases defending ATF and the DEA.[31]

Ramos was persistent. "Who authorized? You were not even informed about it?"

"This is a pretty big government, the United States Government," Obama responded. He smiled. "I've got a lot of moving parts."

"I want to be very clear," Obama continued, "and I spoke to President Calderon when he came to visit just a few weeks ago. Our policy is to ramp up the interdiction of guns flowing south because that's contributing to some of the security problems taking place in Mexico. What we're doing is trying to build the kind of cooperation between Mexico and the United States that we haven't seen before that ensures we have a comprehensive approach," Obama said. "We have to make sure that we're enforcing the kinds of measures that will stop the flow of guns and cash down south that is helping to fuel these transnational drug cartels."[32]

■ ■ ■ ■

In a letter to ATF's acting director Kenneth Melson, Congressman Darrell Issa quoted Senator Grassley to express Congress's frustration with the administration's lack of cooperation in divulging the truth about Fast and Furious. "I'm still asking questions and we're getting the runaround from the Justice Department, [t]hey're stonewalling. The longer the[y] wait, the more they fight, the more egg that they're going to have on their face."[33]

While Senator Grassley urged Attorney General Eric Holder to release all information on Fast and Furious, the Republicans were a minority in the Senate and lacked the power to issue subpoenas on the Judiciary Committee. Grassley therefore could not compel Department of Justice officials to testify. In the House, however, the Republican landslide in the 2010 midterm elections meant, among other things, that Republican Congressman Darrell Issa, the new chairman of the House Committee on Government Oversight and Reform, inherited the gavel of Congress's most potent investigatory arm. Over the next two years, he used its subpoena powers to make dozens of administration officials sweat under the lights of the committee room. One of his signature investigations would be his tenacious pursuit of the facts behind Fast and Furious.

"It's going to be acrimonious, there's no question. [Obama] has been one of the most corrupt presidents in modern times," Issa said on Rush Limbaugh's radio show just before the November 2010 elections. He intended to prove it.

CHAPTER SEVEN

FURY

"You should be ashamed of yourself."

—Congressman Darrell Issa to
Assistant Attorney General Ronald Weich

D arrell Issa was known as a congressional reformer. In 2010 he was honored by the non-partisan Project on Government Oversight for bringing greater transparency to the federal government, including his efforts to release documents from the 2008 AIG bailout and for forming a bipartisan Transparency Caucus in the House of Representatives promoting a more "open and accountable government."[1] The son of Lebanese immigrants who became a self-made millionaire, Issa had dropped out of high school to enlist in the United States Army. Issa earned a GED and later a college degree before forming a hugely successful company that sold car alarms for automobile manufacturers.

Issa began his inquiry into Fast and Furious by asking for documentation about the program from ATF Acting Director Ken Melson. "In the aftermath of the tragic killings of Border Patrol Agent Brian Terry and Immigration and Customs Enforcement Agent Jaime Zapata, it is imperative that you act decisively to assuage the public's deep suspicions that the Bureau of Alcohol, Tobacco, Firearms and Explosives (ATF) has a policy of permitting—and even encouraging—the movement of guns into Mexico by straw purchasers," Issa wrote in a letter dated March 16, 2011.[2] He gave the ATF until the end of the month to provide documents that he and Senator Grassley had requested.

The ATF did not comply with Representative Issa's request.

On April 1, 2011, the House Oversight Committee issued its first subpoena to ATF Acting Director Kenneth Melson. Chairman Issa demanded details about evidence found at Brian Terry's murder scene; whistleblower complaints; handwritten notes about Project Gunrunner; documents and communications between ATF and Lone Wolf Trading company about straw purchaser Jaime Avila; a copy of the presentation given in March 2010 when Holder lieutenant Gary Grindler took notes about the operation; emails about why Fast and Furious was implemented in the first place; and information that detailed the changes made to Project Gunrunner after the inspector general released a report in November 2010 with recommendations for the program. Issa was looking for names—who in the Justice Department approved what appeared to him to be a "fatally stupid" program.[3]

"The unwillingness of this Administration—most specifically the Bureau of Alcohol, Tobacco, and Firearms—to answer questions about this deadly serious matter is deeply troubling," Issa said in a statement.

"Allegations surrounding this program are serious, and the ability of the Justice Department to conduct an impartial investigation is in question. Congressional oversight is necessary to get the truth about what is really happening."[4]

Citing "ongoing investigations," the Justice Department resisted the Republican-led committee's subpoena. As he had with Grassley, Assistant Attorney General Ronald Weich sent a letter brushing off the congressional request. "As we explained, there are some documents that we would be unable to provide without compromising the Department's ongoing criminal investigation into the death of agent Brian Terry as well as other investigations and prosecutions, but we would seek to work productively with the Committee to find other ways to be responsive to its needs," Weich wrote.[5]

Issa was not to be so easily dissuaded. He reminded the Justice Department that Congress was legally entitled to the documents it requested. "Efforts by the Department of Justice and ATF to stonewall the Committee in its investigation by erroneously, but matter-of-factly, citing an internal department policy as a preventative measure for denying access to documents have only enhanced suspicions that such officials have played a role in reckless decisions that have put lives at risk," Issa wrote.[6] If officials did not comply with the congressional subpoena, Issa continued, the Department of Justice would be held in contempt of Congress—a last-recourse measure that would undoubtedly lead to significant political embarrassment for the Obama administration. Since the Watergate scandal in the 1970s, few administration officials have been held in contempt of Congress.

The Issa Committee promptly issued additional subpoenas to officials at both the ATF and the Justice Department. Issa was determined to get Justice Department officials on the record and under oath. In May 2011, he found an ideal opportunity.

On May 3, Attorney General Holder was scheduled to make a standard appearance before the House Judiciary Committee to answer questions about Justice Department activities. Issa is also a member of the Judiciary Committee.

On May 2, the day before his scheduled testimony, Holder and Janet Napolitano visited the White House. Usually when they came to the White House, the two cabinet officials would note in the visitor's log the reason for their visit. On this occasion, they entered the White House together and left together. The White House entry log reads, "No description." The logs show Holder and Napolitano were there to meet with President Obama in the East Room. The Justice Department and Department of Homeland Security have not returned calls for comment.

When Holder appeared before the House Judiciary committee, Issa confronted him on the unfolding scandal.[7]

> **Issa:** When did you first know about the program, officially, I believe, called Fast and Furious? ...
>
> **Holder:** I'm not sure of the exact date but I probably heard about Fast and Furious for the first time over the last few weeks.
>
> **Issa:** Now that you've been briefed on it, the president has said on March 22 that you didn't authorize it. Did your Deputy Attorney General James Cole authorize it?

Holder: I'm sorry the…?

Issa: The Deputy Attorney General James Cole.

Holder: Um… I couldn't hear, did he…?

Issa: Did the deputy attorney general authorize it.

Holder: My guess would be no. Mr. Cole I don't think was in the… I think, I don't think he was in the department at the time that operation started.

Issa: But he's been aware of it much longer.

Holder: Been aware of it much longer?

Issa: Than you have, since you've only been aware of it a few weeks. How about the head of the criminal division Lanny Breuer? Did he authorize it?

Holder: I'm not sure whether Mr. Breuer authorized it…. You have to understand the way in which the department operates. Although there are operations, this one has… gotten a great deal of publicity.

Issa: There are dead Americans as a result of this failed and reckless program so I would say that it hasn't gotten enough attention, has it, Mr. Attorney General.

Holder: ... There's an investigation that is underway.

Issa: I am aware of that investigation.

(crosstalk)

Holder: We'll have to look at that to see exactly ... (crosstalk) I take very seriously the allegation....

Issa: Mr. Attorney General, do you take seriously a subpoena signed by the Clerk of the House?

Holder: Of course.

Issa: After 14 days of waiting for a letter to be signed or acknowledged or responded to, we sent a subpoena signed by the Clerk of the House. 32 days later, last night, your people responded by giving us 92 pages, representing three documents that were public records already, all were available, and saying the other 400 or so responsive pages were not going to be produced. Do you stand by that? And were you aware of that?

Holder: I think we indicated that the other 400 pages would be made available for review, just to be accurate. So those in essence were being made available as well.

Issa: That took 32 days to get that answer.

Holder: The information was gathered as quickly as it could. I've taken steps to enhance our ability to respond to subpoenas and document requests in that regard. I was not satisfied with the pace at which these things were happening, and as I've said, I've taken some steps to make sure that we are more responsive.

Issa: Mr. Attorney General do you agree that Congress has an independent responsibility, particularly when U.S. persons have been killed because of a failed, reckless program, to investigate those who authorized, approved, knew about it and in some other way were responsible for it?

Holder: Well as I indicated to you last night when we spoke about this at the White House, I think that there is a legitimate oversight responsibility that Congress has, but I think also Congress has to use that oversight responsibility in a responsible way. We have cases, 20 matters, that will go to trial in June of this year....

Issa: Mr. Attorney General isn't it true that those cases that will go to trial in June... those cases are basically a bunch of meth addicts who did the buying, that you do not have what this program was supposed to produce. You don't have the kingpins. You don't have the places it [the guns] went. What you have are the people that you already had on videotape many, many months before indictments were brought. Isn't this true?

Holder: There are cases that are important that we are trying to bring that we want to try successfully. They are part of a scheme.... You cannot look at a case as an individual matter and think it's unimportant because small cases lead to larger ones and that's why it is important....

Issa: Mr. Attorney General, my final question though is, from what you're saying about a scheme and so on, do you stand by this program, in other words, and it's not a hypothetical really, if you knew about this program 90 days ago, 180 days ago, would you have allowed it to continue and if not then what are you going to do about the people who did know and allowed it to continue?

Holder: Well what I have told people under the Department of Justice is that under no circumstances in any case, any investigation that we bring should guns be allowed to be distributed in an uncontrolled manner.

Issa: So that would be consistent with the March 9 letter from Deputy Attorney General James Cole in which he said, "We should not design or conduct undercover operations which include guns crossing the border. If we have knowledge that guns are about to cross the border, we must take immediate action to stop the firearms from crossing the border" and so on. That's your policy today?

Holder: That's our policy. That has certainly been the policy that I have tried to impose.

Issa: Isn't Fast and Furious inconsistent with that policy?

Holder: Well that's one of the questions that we'll have to see whether or not Fast and Furious was conducted in a way that's consistent with what Jim [James Cole] wrote there, what I have said today. That's what the inspector general is in fact looking at.

Issa: And would you agree to work with both this committee of course and the other committees investigating this as to, we're not looking at straw buyers, Mr. Attorney General, we're looking at you, straw purchasers. We're looking at you. We're looking at your key people who knew or should have known about this and whether or not your judgment was consistent with good practices and whether or not instead the Justice Department is basically guilty of allowing weapons to kill Americans and Mexicans. So will you agree to cooperate in that investigation both on the House and Senate side?

Holder: We will certainly cooperate with all the investigations but I take great exception to what you just said, the notion that somehow or other this Justice Department is responsible for those deaths that you mentioned, that assertion is offensive....

Issa: What if it's accurate, Mr. Attorney General?

Holder: The Justice Department will do all that it can to protect law enforcement agents. It is one of the reasons why I have tried to look at... a whole variety of methods, techniques that we can use to protect the lives of law enforcement agents, something that this country is not focused enough on....

Issa: What am I going to tell Agent Terry's mother about how he died at the hands of a gun that was videotaped as it was sold to a straw purchaser, fully expecting to end up in the hands of drug cartels.

Holder: ... We'll have to see exactly what happened with regard to guns that are at issue there. I've attended the funerals.... This isn't theoretical, this is not political, this is extremely real for me as Attorney General.... I have had to look into the eyes of widows, of mothers who have lost sons, I have felt their pain, and the notion that somehow, someway we are less than vigilant, less than strong in our determination to keep the people who put their lives on the line everyday to protect the American people, that we're not doing all that we can to protect them is inconsistent with the facts, inconsistent with the people who serve in the Department of Justice.

■ ■ ■ ■ ■

On June 15, 2011, Issa scheduled a full committee hearing on the Fast and Furious scandal. For the first time some of the whistleblowers against the Justice Department and the ATF would detail publicly, under oath, the fatal tactics the ATF had employed.

A day before his testimony, John Dodson was handed a gag order from the Justice Department. The order informed him that he should not speak about details of Fast and Furious lest he risk compromising an internal investigation by the Department's inspector general.

Dodson decided to testify anyway. "Simply put, during this operation known as Fast and Furious, we, ATF, failed to fulfill one of our most fundamental obligations…in part, to keep guns out of the hands of criminals."[8] Dodson disputed the idea that Fast and Furious was a well-intended but "botched" operation. Dodson said, "Allowing loads of weapons that we knew to be destined for criminals, this was the plan." It was, he said, "so mandated."

Another whistleblower, Special Agent Peter Forcelli, told the committee, "As a career law enforcement officer who has had to investigate the deaths of police officers, children, and others at the hands of armed criminals, I was and continue to be horrified [by Operation Fast and Furious]. I believe that these firearms will continue to turn up at crime scenes, on both sides of the border, for years to come."[9]

Also testifying were Brian Terry's mother, Josephine, his sister Michelle, and his cousin Robert Heyer, who not only reminded committee members of the human tragedy of Terry's death but how little the government had been willing to tell them about it.

During questioning, Josephine said she had learned from media reports about the link between Operation Fast and Furious and her son's murder. No one from the government had contacted the family about the ATF's role.[10]

"Most of it I heard from the media. We haven't really gotten anything direct. No direct phone calls or nothing from anybody," she said.[11]

Mrs. Terry was puzzled by the indifference and angry over the revelations. "If they never let the guns walk, maybe Brian would not have been out that day," she said. "I just can't believe our own government came up with a program like this that (let) innocent people get killed."[12]

Robert Heyer gave tear-filled testimony, describing Brian's exemplary life, how much his family missed him, how Brian was taken from them just a few days before Christmas. "It was just ten days before Christmas last year, when our family received the devastating news; Brian had been shot and killed while engaged in a firefight with a group of individuals seeking to do harm to Americans citizens and others."

"The gifts that Brian had picked out with such thought and care began to arrive in the mail that same week. With each delivery, we felt the indescribable pain of Brian's death, but at the same time also remembered his amazing love and spirit."

As he listened to the life of a man he never knew, John Dodson's eyes filled with tears. The entire room grew silent.

Testifying for the Justice Department was Assistant Attorney General Ronald Weich. Congressman Jason Chaffetz of Utah asked Weich if his letters of February 4, 2011, and May 2, 2011, to Senator Grassley, in which Weich said the ATF and the Department of Justice had never allowed gunwalking, were accurate.

Weich said the letters were accurate at the time, but that the Department of Justice was not "clinging" to the information in them.

"So if I said that I think somebody knowingly and willfully, actually misled and lied to Congress," Chaffetz asked, "would I be off-base?"

"Respectfully, Congressman, you would be, in that we make every effort to provide truthful information to Congress."[13]

Chaffetz then noted an internal ATF document, dated January 8, 2010, which stated that the ATF and the Department of Justice had an agreed strategy to continue to allow guns to flow into Mexico. The letter read in part: "Currently our strategy is to allow the transfer of firearms to continue to take place, albeit at a much slower pace, in order to further the investigation and allow for the identification of co-conspirators who would continue to operate and illegally traffic firearms to Mexican DTOs [drug trafficking organizations] which are perpetuating violence along the Southwest border."[14]

Chaffetz pressed on.

Chaffetz: I want to know when the Attorney General actually got engaged in this. Why didn't he know about it? When did he know about it? Or was he just oblivious to it?

Weich: ... [Holder] answered Chairman Issa's question on the House Judiciary Committee. The question was ....

Chaffetz: But I questioned him, also, on the House Judiciary Committee, if you remember. You were sitting in the row right behind him.... And he said he didn't know when he first knew about it. So I'm trying to figure out, when did he know about it? And then what did he do about it?

Weich: He told Congressman Issa that he first learned about it several weeks before the hearing in connection with a press report.

Chaffetz: And what I don't understand is, when you go back and look at the record, President Obama knew about it back in March. If the President knew about it, why didn't the Attorney General know about it? And why are you issuing a memo in May, when the President of the United States, in an interview with, I believe, Univision, is saying we know that there were some mistakes made? How does that happen? The President makes this comment, and then, still, months later, you have the gall to issue a memo to this Congress saying, that is just false, it is not true. That does not add up.[15]

At one point in the hearing, Chairman Issa held up the heavily redacted documents—some pages completely blacked out—that the Justice Department had finally submitted to the Committee. "Sir, if you are going to count pages like this as discovery, you should be ashamed of yourself," he said. "You have given us black paper instead of white paper. You might as well have given us a ream still in its original binder."

Dennis Burke testified to the House Oversight Committee behind closed doors, but part of his testimony was released by Democratic Ranking Member Elijah Cummings:

Border Patrol Agent Brian Terry was killed on December 15, 2011, by Mexican bandits in the Arizona desert. The men killed him using high-powered weapons provided by the Obama Justice Department through Operation Fast and Furious.

Photo: AP Images

Thousands of these types of "assault weapons" were knowingly sold to Mexican drug cartels through Operation Fast and Furious by the United States government. Local police forces, sheriff departments, and the Border Patrol don't have this kind of firepower.

Photo: AP Images/Matt York

ATF Special Agent and whistleblower John Dodson stands in the Arizona desert not far from where Brian Terry was murdered with guns given to Mexican drug cartel members by his agency. *Photo: AP Images/Matt York*

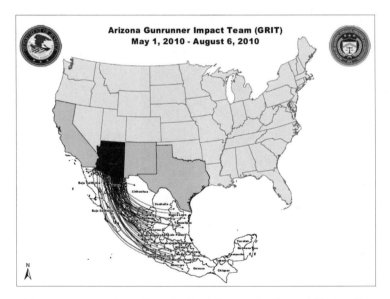

Arizona Gunrunner Impact Team (GRIT)
May 1, 2010 - August 6, 2010

This map was sent from Phoenix Special Agent in Charge Bill Newell to White House National Security Advisor Kevin O'Reilly in 2010. The map shows how guns from Arizona were showing up at violent crime scenes in Mexico. *Credit: U.S. Department of Justice*

ATF Special Agent in Charge of the Phoenix Field Division Bill Newell holds a press conference announcing the indictment of straw purchasers. Newell said he believed that straw purchasers have "just as much blood on their hands as the criminals who use them." Former Arizona U.S. Attorney Dennis Burke is shown to Newell's left.

Photo: AP Images/Matt York

Two of Homeland Security Secretary Janet Napolitano's agents were killed with weapons that went to Mexico under Operation Fast and Furious, yet she says she never talked about Fast and Furious with Attorney General Eric Holder.

Photo: AP Images/Haraz N. Ghanbari

Despite being sent memos discussing Fast and Furious as early as summer 2010, Attorney General Eric Holder claims he has only known about the program since February 2011. *Photo: AP Images/J. Scott Applewhite*

Attorney General Eric Holder receives advice and counsel from Assistant Attorney General Ronald Weich during a congressional hearing. Weich often gave Holder tips about what to say when he was questioned about Operation Fast and Furious under oath. A letter Weich sent to Congress regarding Fast and Furious had to be withdrawn because it was so misleading and false. *Photo: AP Images/Susan Walsh*

Republican Senator Charles Grassley, left, the first member of Congress to investigate Operation Fast and Furious, stands with Attorney General Eric Holder and Democratic Senator Patrick Leahy. *Photo: © J. Scott Applewhite/ /AP/Corbis*

Deputy Attorney General Lanny Breuer of the Department of Justice Criminal Division testifies before Congress about Operation Fast and Furious. After nearly a year of denial, Breuer finally admitted to knowing about "gunwalking" at the ATF. Breuer served in private practice with Eric Holder and now serves as Holder's number two man in the Justice Department. Breuer also approved detailed wiretap applications for Operation Fast and Furious in early 2010. *Photo: AP Images/J. Scott Applewhite*

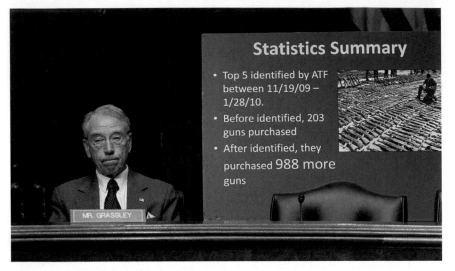

Senator Charles Grassley shows statistics about Operation Fast and Furious, revealing ATF had identified multiple straw purchasers a year before Brian Terry was killed, and that purchasers were allowed to continue purchasing weapons after being identified. *Photo: AP Images/J. Scott Applewhite*

Chairman of the House Committee on Oversight and Government Reform Darrell Issa speaks during a congressional hearing about Operation Fast and Furious. Issa has issued multiple subpoenas, but has been stonewalled by the Obama Justice Department. *Photo: AP Images/Susan Walsh*

Chairman Issa speaks with House Oversight Committee ranking member Democrat Elijah Cummings. Cummings has repeatedly called for more gun control in light of Operation Fast and Furious. *Photo: AP Images/J. Scott Applewhite*

Mexican Attorney General Marisela Morales was left in the dark about Operation Fast and Furious. She has called for officials involved in the operation to be extradited from the U.S. and sent to Mexico for prosecution. *Photo: AP Images/Eduardo Verdugo*

Arizona Governor Jan Brewer has been at war with the Obama administration over border security for more than three years. Brewer has said she is "outraged" by Fast and Furious, and that the program "endangered the lives of innocent people on both sides of the border." *Photo: AP Images/Ross D. Franklin*

President Barack Obama has refused to take responsibility for Operation Fast and Furious. Obama maintains he has "full faith and confidence" in Attorney General Eric Holder and his handling of the scandal.

Photo: AP Images/Rex Features

I take responsibility. I'm not going to say mistakes were made. I'm going to say we made mistakes. I am the United States Attorney for the District of Arizona.

I get to stand up when we have a great case to announce and take all the credit for it regardless of how much work I did on it. So when our office makes mistakes, I need to take responsibility, and this is a case, as reflected by the work of this investigation, it should not have been done the way it was done, and I want to take responsibility for that, and I'm not falling on a sword or trying to cover for anyone else.

I think that's literally how the system operates, which is I'm the chief law enforcement officer, Federal law enforcement officer for the District of Arizona. ATF doesn't report to me, FBI doesn't report to me, DEA doesn't report to me or CBP [U.S. Customs and Border Protection]. With that said, if investigations are conducted in my district and that have gotten to the prosecution stage, I have a responsibility regardless of what I knew or when, I want the record to reflect that I really want to take responsibility for anything that occurred in this case and faults and what we can learn to do better in the future on cases like this.[16]

Burke appeared to be the administration's sacrificial lamb. He denied, however, that he knew anything about the Justice Department authorizing gunwalking as a strategy.

Q: Did anyone from Main Justice, from the Justice Department headquarters, ever come down and tell you there is in fact a different policy that we are going to allow guns to go across the border in order to build bigger cases?

A: No.

Q: Did anyone ever discuss—from the Department of Justice main headquarters—your supervisors—ever discuss with you or raise to your attention that there was a new policy with respect to interdiction of weapons or surveillance of firearms?

A: No. Not that I can recall at all.

Q: And did anyone ever—from the Department of Justice, Main Justice I will call it, ever tell you that you were authorized to allow weapons to cross the border when you otherwise would have had a legal authority to seize or interdict them because they were a suspected straw purchase or it was suspected that they were being trafficked in a firearms scheme?

A: I have no recollection of ever being told that.

In July, however, in secret testimony to Issa and his staff, Acting ATF Director Kenneth Melson—who for months had been blocked by the Justice Department from testifying, but was finally informed he was allowed to do so outside of his official capacity with a personal lawyer[17]—confirmed the Justice Department's involvement in

Operation Fast and Furious. He also confirmed suspicions that informants with the Drug Enforcement Agency (DEA) and the FBI had been involved and said there was a "smoking gun" report detailing who in the Justice Department approved the wiretaps and tactics for Fast and Furious.

Chairman Issa was surprised by his interview with Melson, who distanced himself from the Justice Department. Melson reportedly became physically ill discussing the gruesome details of Fast and Furious and the tactics his bureau had approved. He revealed that the reason the Justice Department seemed unwilling cooperate with the House Oversight investigation into Fast and Furious was simply because the wagons were being circled around President Obama's political appointees. "It was very frustrating to all of us, and it appears thoroughly to us that the Department is really trying to figure out a way to push the information away from their political appointees at the Department," Melson said.[18]

In response to Melson's testimony, Congressman Issa and Senator Grassley wrote a joint letter to Justice Department officials. "The Department should not be withholding what Mr. Melson described as the 'smoking gun' report of investigation or Mr. Melson's emails regarding the wiretap applications," the letter stated. "Mr. Melson said he reviewed the affidavits in support of the wiretap applications for the first time after the controversy became public and immediately contacted the Deputy Attorney General's office to raise concerns about information in them that was inconsistent with the Department's public denials. The Department should also address the serious questions raised by Mr. Melson's testimony regarding potential informants for other agencies."

A month before information about Melson's closed door testimony became public, rumors swirled that Melson was being forced to resign as acting head of the ATF. (He was eventually reassigned elsewhere in the Justice Department.)

In August 2011, U.S. Attorney Dennis Burke tendered his resignation. Janet Napolitano's longtime confidante said that "it is the right time to move on to pursue other aspects of my career and my life and allow the office to move ahead." Burke didn't mention Fast and Furious as a reason for his departure.

The resignation led Attorney General Holder to issue a statement praising Burke's leadership. "I am grateful to Dennis for his dedication and service to the Department of Justice over these many years and commend his decision to place the interests of the U.S. Attorney's Office above all else."

Then Burke all but disappeared. As his hometown newspaper, the *Arizona Republic* put it, "Since that day, the gregarious public servant has gone silent, and nearly invisible, except that his name appears prominently in Justice Department documents, congressional hearings and news reports."[19] The paper called Burke's downfall "shocking." Issa's investigation had apparently led to the fall of two designated fall guys. The congressman, however, was not satisfied. "While the reckless disregard for safety that took place in Operation Fast and Furious certainly merits changes within the Department of Justice, the Oversight and Government Reform Committee will continue its investigation to ensure that blame isn't offloaded on just a few individuals for a matter that involved much higher levels of the Justice Department," Issa said in a statement.

■ ■ ■ ■ ■

On October 21, 2010, the brother of Chihuahua Attorney General Patricia Gonzalez Rodriguez, Mario Gonzalez Rodriguez, a high profile lawyer, was kidnapped by members of the Juarez drug cartel. A photo has since surfaced of Mario kneeling with his hands and feet bound, surrounded by cartel members in camouflage, masks, bullet proof vests, and combat boots, armed to the teeth with assault rifles. Under extreme torture, Mario accused his sister, Miss Patricia Gonzalez, of ordering killings on behalf of the cartel. Miss Gonzalez denied the allegations and accused the Juarez cartel of getting revenge for prosecutions her office had made against the Sinaloa Cartel and corrupt Mexican government officials who were in bed with them.

Fifteen days later, Mario's body was found in a makeshift grave. His murder sparked a major firefight between the Mexican federal police and cartel members. Eight members were arrested, and sixteen weapons were seized. Two of them were Fast and Furious guns.[20]

In June 2011, Carlos Canino, the ATF's Deputy Attaché to Mexico, contacted Mexico's attorney general, Marisela Morales. Canino decided he could no longer keep secret that his agency likely had been responsible for the deaths of dozens of Mexican citizens, and responsible for giving guns to the killers of Mario Gonzalez Rodriguez. "If I hadn't told the Attorney General this, and this had come out in the news media, I would never be able to work with her ever again," Canino explained, "and we would be done in Mexico."[21]

Morales had heard about Fast and Furious sporadically from American media reports following Brian Terry's murder, but she didn't know the gruesome details until informed by Canino.

"*Hijole*," Morales responded, the Spanish version of "Oh my," when she learned about the Fast and Furious operation.

Her shock soon turned to anger. "In no way would we have allowed [this operation]," she later told the *Los Angeles Times*, "because it is an attack on the safety of Mexicans."[22]

It was estimated that hundreds of Mexicans had been killed with guns linked to Operation Fast and Furious, and that many more will suffer a violent fate in the future. Morales called for the extradition of those responsible. If they would not face justice in the United States, they would face justice in her country. "We're going to get to the bottom of this and we're going to punish…whoever is responsible for these crimes," she said to applause, during an address to the lower house of the Mexican Congress.[23]

The Mexican attorney general reportedly requested that at least three individuals involved in Fast and Furious to be sent to Mexico to answer questions. The identities of those individuals are still not known.

Darren Gil, the former head of the ATF contingent in Mexico who had tried to shut the program down, offered a public apology to the Mexican government for his role in the enterprise. "I hope they understand that this operation was kept secret from most of ATF, including me and my colleagues in Mexico," Gil said during congressional testimony. "Unfortunately, as a result of this operation, it is the Mexican people who will continue to suffer the consequences of narco-terrorism related firearms violence. I have no doubt, as recent media reports have indicated, that American citizens will also be exposed to more firearms-related violence as a result of this operation."[24]

Just as the Fast and Furious scandal threatened to become a major international incident—and intensely embarrassing to the Obama administration, which had worked hard to form an alliance with Mexico's government—the outcry suddenly softened.

On August 15, 2011, William Burns, America's Deputy Secretary of State, traveled to Mexico to meet with Mexico's Foreign Secretary, Patricia Espinoza.[25] According to an inside source who spoke to me only on condition of anonymity, Burns gave the Mexican government an ultimatum: mute its criticism of Fast and Furious or give up a $500 million payment through the Merida Initiative, a State Department program providing funding to combat drug trafficking and related violence.[26] Former Secretary of State Condoleezza Rice called the Merida Initiative "one of the most important initiatives the United States, Mexico and Central America have ever launched." The money is spent on equipment, training, and economic and social development programs to fight gang and cartel crime. After that meeting, official outrage from the Mexican government seemed to abate.

The Mexican government may have been persuaded to change the subject, but the United States Congress was just getting going.

CHAPTER EIGHT

PAYBACK

"There are many people that I know of still with firsthand information about this case who want to cooperate, have expressed that to me, that have information that they feel you need to further your investigation, but are afraid of ATF and retaliation for talking to you...."[1]

—ATF Agent #2

In 1986, Congress passed the Whistleblower Act and the No Fear Act. The two laws were designed to protect from retaliation whistleblowers coming forward with information about corruption or illegality within the government. But for years, the department tasked with enforcing whistleblower protection laws, the Justice Department, has been exceedingly lax when those laws have been applied to its own operations.

The ATF, in particular, was notable in this regard. That was especially true in the Phoenix office where Bill Newell's vindictive treatment of Special Agent Jay Dobyns—the highly decorated agent who had infiltrated the Hells Angels and who had called Newell out for failing to act on credible threats against himself and his family—was notorious. Though two separate federal reports on the incident had found the Phoenix office culpable for not protecting Dobyns, Newell's superiors in Washington did not reprimand him; instead they entrusted him with the major operation that became Fast and Furious.

"ATF wasn't going to do anything to Bill Newell. They were going to defend and protect him because he was their golden boy," Dobyns said. "The identical techniques, tactics, practices and personnel that were used on me were repeated in Fast and Furious. You go into the immediate denial of 'no we didn't do that.' Then, when it starts to be proved, you go into the attack on the person that exposed it, that blew the whistle."[2]

■ ■ ■ ■ ■

When John Dodson complained to management at the ATF field office in Phoenix about the failure to arrest the straw buyers that his Group VII had been monitoring as part of Fast and Furious, Assistant Special Agent in Charge George Gillett made it clear that any agent who wanted a career with the ATF would stay away from Dodson and deny gunwalking allegations.

Dodson's rifle was taken away[3] and he was no longer allowed to participate in operations. David Voth, one of his supervisors, demanded unnecessary written reports detailing his daily activities.[4] First, Dodson was transferred to surveillance duty, where he watched video cameras for ten hours a day in a dark closet; then he was ordered to turn in his ATF badge and transfer to the FBI's office in Phoenix, where he would be prohibited from working on any cases involving his former agency.

While at the FBI, Dodson investigated a Nigerian arms smuggling ring. When he found dozens of 9mm handguns and Mossberg shotguns wrapped and ready to be shipped, Dodson had to notify the ATF. Any suspected international firearms trafficking fell solely under the jurisdiction of ATF, and his old Group VII specialized in combating trafficking. He called his former supervisors.

"This is your ugly baby," David Voth allegedly told Dodson. "I'm not helping you."[5]

It was after a year of retaliatory treatment from his ATF supervisors that Dodson gave evidence to congressional investigators in Washington, D.C., about the details of Fast and Furious. When he returned to the Phoenix Field Division and refused orders from his superiors to retract his testimony, he was confronted by George Gillett, who, in the middle of a corridor, with other agents present, screamed that any agent who communicated with Dodson would find it detrimental to his ATF career.[6] The party line, echoed initially by ATF Director Ken Melson when allegations about Fast and Furious first surfaced, was that Dodson was just a disgruntled employee. That portrayal wouldn't bear scrutiny as the whistleblowers' evidence mounted.

■ ■ ■ ■ ■

Growing up, Vince Cefalu always wanted to be a cop. "I read everything cop. I bought everything cop. I ate, slept, and drank cop."[7] Cefalu admired Detective Frank Serpico, a New York City police officer who exposed police corruption in that city. Testifying before the Knapp Commission in 1971, Detective Serpico said:

Through my appearance here today...I hope that police officers in the future will not experience the same frustration and anxiety that I was subjected to for the past five years at the hands of my superiors because of my attempt to report corruption....We create an atmosphere in which the honest officer fears the dishonest officer, and not the other way around....The problem is that the atmosphere does not yet exist in which honest police officers can act without fear of ridicule or reprisal from fellow officers.[8]

Cefalu saw Serpico as a role model—someone who did the right thing, no matter the personal cost—and held himself to the same standards of professional integrity. "None of us Fast and Furious whistleblowers thought we would experience many of the same corrupt tactics, abuses, and choices 40 years after Serpico testified as a whistleblower on police corruption at the New York City Knapp Commission hearings,"[9] Cefalu says.

For the majority of his career, Cefalu was known as a "go-to guy" in the ATF. A superb investigator, he received nothing but the highest evaluations. Because of his dedication and ability to get things done, Cefalu was promoted through the ranks quickly, becoming a top special agent.

When he discovered that ATF agents were circumventing the process for getting wiretaps approved, he reported it to his supervisors. He was told to either ignore the problem or be reassigned to Fargo, North Dakota. Cefalu filed an ethics complaint; in return, his supervisors labeled him a disgruntled employee.

When he tried to report evidence of misconduct regarding the misuse of wiretaps to more senior management in Washington, he was accused of insubordination. "If you ever jump your chain of command again, you will face severe consequences," Cefalu says he was told.

On January 17, 2006, Cefalu's supervisors officially accused him of misconduct. This was followed by six official reprimands, two suspensions, and attempts to demonstrate Cefalu was not fit for duty. He was told he needed to undergo a psychiatric evaluation. Cefalu was transferred five times and given two "termination proposals"—what he described as "a proposal for removal for telling the truth."[10] He was sent on year-long assignments away from his family. He was pulled from field assignments and tied to a desk job, which made no use of his specialized skills (working undercover, negotiating hostage situations, or pulling hard criminals off the streets), which ATF had once praised. The ATF internal affairs division critiqued everything he did in an effort, Cefalu believed, to get him to quit. After five years of the ATF "investigating" (or harassing) Cefalu, he was cleared of any wrongdoing. His ATF file is clean.

Cefalu said that many of the apparently retaliatory actions taken against him "were reviewed, sanctioned, or approved by senior members of ATF management staff whom I had made formal allegations against."[11]

But Cefalu says the worst part wasn't even the direct retaliation from the supervisors. Instead, it was friends and partners in the bureau, people he had known for as long as twenty years, ignoring him, avoiding him. They had gotten the message: "If you're seen with Vince, your career is over too."

Cefalu learned that his case was not unusual, that the ATF routinely went after whistleblowers. He co-founded CleanUpATF.org, an online forum where agents could expose corruption within the bureau. Stories of mismanagement flooded in.

"Senior managers were alleged to be engaged in inter-office affairs with subordinate employees, attending strip clubs at lunch, releasing sensitive law enforcement information, lying under oath," and other misdeeds.[12] Cefalu said that through CleanUpATF.org, he had a network of whistleblowing agents and inspectors. When he received reports about scandals linked to Fast and Furious, "I took this information to Congress and advocated others to do the same." Still an ATF agent, he also presented these allegations to Acting ATF Director Melson, but was ignored, even though public controversy about Fast and Furious was growing rapidly. Cefalu covered Fast and Furious revelations on his website and accepted invitations to talk about the scandal on Fox News and other major media outlets.

In June 2011, Cefalu's supervisors told him to turn in his gun and took away his badge. ATF attorneys implied he was being investigated for misconduct, but Vince knew better; he was being punished for his efforts to expose wrongdoing in Operation Fast and Furious. Department of Justice attorneys threatened to shut down CleanUpATF.org.

Cefalu has since filed a lawsuit in California charging the ATF with unlawful retaliation against a whistleblower.

■ ■ ■ ■ ■

Peter Forcelli joined the ATF's New York division in June 2001 after fourteen years' service in the NYPD. In May 2007 he became Group

Supervisor in the Phoenix field office. Four years later, he was the first whistleblower to detail the role the U.S. Attorney's Office played in Fast and Furious before Congress. He explained that solid gunrunning cases with unimpeachable evidence had been regularly dropped for years. He never found a valid explanation for the failure to prosecute.

"This operation, which in my opinion endangered the American public, was orchestrated in conjunction with Assistant U.S. Attorney Emory Hurley," Forcelli said under oath to the Issa Committee on June 15, 2011. "I have read documents that indicate that his boss, U.S. Attorney Dennis Burke, also agreed with the direction of the case."

After his testimony, the U.S. Attorney's Office in Arizona decided to reopen a case Forcelli had been involved in three years earlier. His superiors conveniently accused him of lying about the case and case evidence. Before Forcelli turned over evidence against the Fast and Furious operation, the U.S. attorney had found insufficient evidence to pursue the case at all, but was now opening it up simply to target Forcelli. Other agents at ATF were instructed to report any conversations or contact with Forcelli to their supervisors.[13]

Forcelli was given what he says is a do-nothing job that makes no use of his talents. He requested reassignment away from the Arizona U.S. Attorney's Office and now works in ATF headquarters.

"I will fight for my integrity. I was an agent in New York during 9/11. I have a life-long illness as a result of my work at that site. As a cop, as a detective, and even as an agent my kids were growing up. Christmas, I'd be out working homicide cases. I didn't see my kids open their gifts year after year after year. I missed my kids' childhood, I sacrificed my health, they will not take my integrity. That I will not give them," he said. "They have no idea what this has done to my wife, my kids, my life has been turned upside down," he said.

Not only is ATF intimidation ruining the lives of brave whistleblowers who stood up for the truth, but it also has cost taxpayers hundreds of thousands of dollars, if not millions. On average, it costs $100,000 to relocate a single agent. It costs taxpayers nearly $10,000 an hour for ATF investigators to interview so-called "rogue" agents like Cefalu.

Congressman Issa expressed outrage over the retaliatory efforts against well-regarded agents who were simply trying to bring the truth to light. "These statements reveal a worrying cycle: a history of retaliation by ATF management causes its employees to fear reprisals, which in turn prevents them from coming forward to the Committee," he wrote in a letter to the ATF. "This needs to end." Senator Grassley described the treatment of whistleblowers by the ATF and Justice Department as making them feel like "a skunk at a picnic for simply telling the truth."[14]

Joined by three other members of Congress, Issa introduced legislation to reinforce provisions of the 1989 Whistleblower Protection Act. The Whistleblower Protection Enhancement Act is designed to close loopholes in the original law and prohibit gag orders like the one the ATF and Justice Department had placed on John Dodson in the hours before his testimony to Congress.

Numerous anonymous agents have told Issa that they want to come forward with more information about Fast and Furious, but that they fear for their careers, which could be harmed through reassignment, disciplinary actions, or other retaliatory measures. "There are many people that I know of still with firsthand information about this case who want to cooperate," one agent told Issa, "that have information that they feel you need to further your investigation, but are afraid of ATF and retaliation for talking to you."[15]

Even without such information, the case against the administration in its conduct and cover-up of Fast and Furious was becoming undeniable.

CHAPTER NINE

REVELATIONS

"It isn't the original scandal that gets people in the most trouble—it's the attempted cover-up."

—Congressman Tom Petri

On July 26, 2011, Issa's House Committee on Government Oversight and Reform held another hearing. The Committee was still being denied thousands of documents from the Justice Department and had still not established how many senior government executives had authorized Operation Fast and Furious or why.

ATF agents who had been stationed in Mexico and ATF Phoenix field office managers were called to testify under oath. Former Attaché to Mexico Darren Gil, and his successor Carlos Canino, both confirmed that they had been ordered to keep Mexican officials in the dark about the agency's project to walk 2,500 guns into their country.

Bill Newell offered the day's most important revelations. As the head of the Phoenix office, Newell had been the manager charged with overseeing the execution of Fast and Furious, the operation he once called "historic." Newell was unrepentant. In front of the committee, Newell revealed publicly for the first time that Fast and Furious was not just an ATF and Department of Justice operation, but had involved the Internal Revenue Service, Immigration and Customs Enforcement, the Department of Homeland Security, and the Drug Enforcement Administration. According to Newell, "A case like Fast and Furious goes through several levels of approval."[1]

Newell also admitted that he had spoken to Kevin O'Reilly, a senior staffer on Obama's National Security Council (NSC), about Operation Fast and Furious. The two men had been longtime friends. During Fast and Furious, O'Reilly served as the NSC's Director of North American Affairs. He also had been a former top aide to Secretary of State Hillary Clinton. It was Issa who prompted Newell to make the revelation about O'Reilly, who was the first White House official to be directly linked to knowledge of Fast and Furious.

"Did you talk to him about this case?" Issa asked Newell.

"I might have talked to him about this case. Yes, sir."

"Do you know when that was?"

"It was probably—I—as I recall I think it was during the sum-mer—it might have been the summer or early fall of 2010."

Emails surrendered to the Issa Committee confirmed the com-munications. In a September 3, 2010, email to O'Reilly, Newell wrote, "You didn't get these from me.... The second Word doc is what we were going to give to ATF DD Melson as notes in case he got asked specific questions about our industry Operations efforts during GRIT."[2]

"GRIT" referred to a "gunrunner impact team." Four new GRIT teams were developed as part of the Southwest Border Initiative. John

Dodson's Group VII was the GRIT team assigned to Fast and Furious. The email continued:

> Also, not mentioned in these docs but VERY relevant to Mr. Brennan's meeting next week is the fact that we and the USA[U.S. attorney] were going to announce the indictment of a dozen "straw purchaser" case [*sic*] addressing firearms trafficking by 30 individuals. We finally have the USAO [U.S. Attorney's Office] here on board with going after "straw" purchasers and making a statement, publically especially, that we will take action against those folks.

The emails, released by the White House in response to congressional subpoena, undercut Newell's claim to the committee that "at no time in our strategy was it to allow guns to be taken to Mexico." One of the emails, in fact, included a map showing exactly where the guns from the Phoenix areas were showing up in Mexico.

"This 'arrow' chart reflects the criminal investigation side of GRIT," Newell wrote on September 3, 2010. "Each arrow represents the ultimate destination of firearms we intercepted and/or where the guns ended up through firearms tracing we were able to initiate criminal investigations."[3]

"The arrow chart is really interesting—and—no surprise—implies at least that different DTO [drug trafficking] organizations in Mx [Mexico] have very different and geographically distinct networks in the U.S. for acquiring guns," O'Reilly replied.[4] Emails also indicate the two spoke on the phone.

O'Reilly wasn't the only one in the White House with information from Newell. He forwarded information about Fast and Furious to Special Assistant to the President Dan Restrepo, and Director for Terrorist Finance and Counternarcotics Greg Gatjanis.[5] Issa promptly requested all communications from O'Reilly, Restrepo, and Gatjanis regarding Project Gunrunner and Operation Fast and Furious memos, emails, briefing papers, and handwritten notes. In addition, Issa demanded an interview with O'Reilly.

An Obama administration source told CBS News that White House national security staffers were "briefed on the toplines of ongoing federal efforts, but nobody in [the] White House knew about the investigative tactics being used in the operation, let alone any decision to let guns walk." Newell's email to O'Reilly, however, implied otherwise.

Within weeks of Newell's testimony, O'Reilly was transferred to Iraq. He was to become the State Department's new director of the International Narcotics and Law Enforcement Bureau there. He has been called to testify before Issa's committee, but the chairman has been told that because of his overseas assignment, O'Reilly is not available for questioning.

During the congressional summer recess, the Justice Department issued a statement confirming then denying that at least eleven crimes were committed on American soil in 2011 with guns traceable to Fast and Furious. The Justice Department provided no details except to say the crimes occurred in Phoenix and El Paso. The ATF soon followed up with a startling statistic: 800 of the 2,500 guns were linked to criminal activity in the United States and Mexico.[6]

These revelations did not prevent the promotion of some of the leaders of Operation Fast and Furious. In early August 2011, it was announced that Bill Newell had been promoted to ATF headquarters as a special assistant to the assistant director of the agency's Office of Management, and Fast and Furious Supervisor David Voth, who had a habit of threatening subordinates and directly oversaw straw purchasing, was offered a promotion in ATF's Tobacco Division.

■ ■ ■ ■ ■

Meanwhile, Attorney General Holder, their ultimate boss, was finding that his testimony denying any knowledge of Fast and Furious before it was reported in the newspapers was fast unraveling.

On October 3, 2011, the Justice Department finally released a tranche of long-sought documents. Among them were memos demonstrating that Attorney General Holder was briefed on Operation Fast and Furious on a regular basis starting as early as July 5, 2010. According to the documents, Holder was briefed at least five times on the program:

> To: The Attorney General
> From: Michael F. Walther Director National Drug Intelligence Center
>
> Subject: Weekly Report from July 5 through July 9, 2010
>
> Field Division with its investigation of Manuel Celis-Acosta as part of OCDETF Operation Fast and Furious. This investigation, initiated in September 2009 in conjunction with the Drug Enforcement Administration, Immigration and

Customs Enforcement, and the Phoenix Police Department, involves a Phoenix-based firearms trafficking ring headed by Manuel Celis-Acosta. Celis-Acosta and (redacted) straw purchasers are responsible for the purchase of 1,500 firearms that were then supplied to Mexican drug trafficking cartels. They also have direct ties to the Sinaloa Cartel, which is suspected of providing $1 million for the purchase of firearms in the greater Phoenix area.[7]

Another memo was submitted to Holder from his number two man at the Department, Deputy Attorney General Lanny Breuer:

To: The Attorney General
The Acting Deputy Attorney General

From: Lanny A. Breuer
Assistant Attorney General

Date: Week of November 1, 2010
Re: Weekly Reports

Phoenix-based "Operation Fast and Furious," is ready for takedown.[8]

Issa wrote a scathing letter to Holder outlining what he said were a pattern of Justice Department denials of wrongdoing or gunwalking, which were revised only after Congress forced new information to light:

Once documentary and testimonial evidence strongly contradicted these claims, the Department attempted to limit the fallout from Fast and Furious to the Phoenix Field Division of the Bureau of Alcohol, Tobacco, Firearms, and Explosives (ATF). When that effort also proved unsuccessful, the Department next argued that Fast and Furious resided only within ATF itself, before eventually also assigning blame to the U.S. Attorney's Office in Arizona.

Just last month, you claimed that Fast and Furious did not reach the upper levels of the Justice Department. Documents discovered through the course of the investigation, however, have proved each and every one of these claims advanced by the Department to be untrue.[9]

Holder responded by saying he never read the memos and blamed his staff for failing to inform him about Fast and Furious. To "clarify" his earlier testimony, Holder sent a letter to the House Oversight Committee:

Much has been made in the past few days about my congressional testimony earlier this year regarding Fast and Furious. My testimony was truthful and accurate and I have been consistent on this point throughout. I have no recollection of knowing about Fast and Furious or hearing its name prior to the public controversy about it. Prior to early 2011, I certainly never knew about the tactics employed in the operation and it is my understanding that the former United States Attorney for the District of Arizona and the

former Acting Director and Deputy Director of ATF have
told Congress that they, themselves, were unaware of the
tactics employed.[10]

Congressman Issa, among many other members of Congress, found
the claims unpersuasive. "It appears your latest defense has reached a
new low," Issa told Holder. "You now claim that you were unaware of
Fast and Furious because your staff failed to inform you of information
contained in memos that were specifically addressed to you. At best,
this indicates negligence and incompetence in your duties as Attorney
General. At worst, it places your credibility into serious doubt."[11]

Other congressional investigators weren't buying Holder's story
either. Arizona Congressman Paul Gosar, who sits on the House Oversight Committee with Chairman Issa, told me that Holder's position
was untenable, saying of the attorney general, "If you didn't know, it's
even worse that you didn't know—that you allowed this to occur on
your watch. It shows a government out of control."[12]

The White House came to Holder's defense. "The bottom line is
the Attorney General's testimony to both the House and the Senate
was consistent and truthful," White House Press Secretary Jay Carney
told reporters during an October 2011 briefing. "He said in both
March and May of this year that he became aware of the questionable
tactics deployed in the Fast and Furious Operation in early 2011
when ATF agents first raised them publicly. He then asked the inspector general to investigate the matter, demonstrating how seriously
they took them."[13] President Obama told reporters, "I have complete
confidence in Attorney General Holder, in how he handles his
office."[14]

Issa commented later, "The President has said he has full confidence in this attorney general. I have no confidence in a president who has confidence in an attorney general who has in fact not terminated or dealt with the individuals, including key lieutenants who from the very beginning had some knowledge and long before Brian Terry was gunned down, knew enough to stop this program."[15]

The Oversight Committee issued a new round of subpoenas. Issa expanded his inquiry from communications about Fast and Furious within the Justice Department to communications between Department of Justice employees and the Office of the President about the operation. He wanted documents relating to Obama's March 22, 2011, interview with Univision, when he denied knowing about Fast and Furious, and claimed the government had a lot of "moving parts." Issa wanted to know what Obama was coached to say if the topic of Fast and Furious came up in that interview.

Shortly after the subpoenas were issued, Deputy Attorney General of the Criminal Division Lanny Breuer, the man responsible for approving wiretap applications, including those in Fast and Furious, admitted during a Senate Judiciary Committee hearing that he in fact knew that gunwalking tactics were being used during Fast and Furious as early as April 2010, but that he failed to inform his boss, Holder, about the details. Assistant Attorney General Ronald Weich tried to pin gunwalking tactics on a Bush administration program known as Wide Receiver, which was stopped immediately when guns were lost.[16] Breuer misleadingly labeled Fast and Furious by its Bush-era predecessor.

"Knowing what I now know was a pattern of unacceptable and misguided tactics used by the ATF, I regret that I did not alert others within the leadership of the Department of Justice to the tactics used in Operation Wide Receiver when they first came to my attention," Breuer said in a statement.

Breuer's statement contradicted the original letter the Justice Department sent to Senator Charles Grassley in February 2011 denying gunwalking allegations. Perhaps it was telling that Breuer had overseen the letter's drafting but had someone else—Assistant Attorney General Ronald Weich—sign it. The Department informed Senator Grassley's office that the original letter was hereby "withdrawn,"[17] a rare and nearly unheard of occurrence.

In response to Breuer's startling admission that he was, in fact, aware of gunwalking by the ATF, Senator Grassley went to the floor of the Senate and demanded Breuer's resignation. "The Justice Department had publicly denied to Congress that ATF would ever walk guns," Grassley said. "Yet the head of the Criminal Division, Mr. Breuer knew otherwise and said nothing."[18]

For ATF whistleblowers, Breuer's belated admission was a moment of vindication and anger.

"We were called liars in the beginning," Special Agent Peter Forcelli stated. "Then you have Lanny Breuer come out recently and say 'well we knew, before those guys came forward we knew.' That's horrific."[19]

Attorney General Holder, however, remained unfazed. "I cannot be expected to know the details of every operation," he said.[20]

On November 8, 2011, Holder appeared before the Senate Judiciary Committee, where he faced hard questions from Senator Grassley and Texas Senator John Cornyn. The room was tense and crammed. There were reporters from Mexico sitting at the press table, anxiously waiting Holder's arrival. More than fifty congressmen had called for Holder's resignation, and the press had caught on that Holder might have committed perjury. "I first learned about the tactics at the beginning of this year," Holder said during the hearing. "In my testimony before the house committee [in May] I did say [I first learned about it] a few weeks [before], I probably should have said a couple of months."[21] Visibly frustrated, Holder said the focus on his conflicting testimony regarding when he knew about Operation Fast and Furious was a "distraction."

Senator Cornyn confronted Holder with a timeline of his statements and about the false February 2011 letter his department submitted to Congress.

> **Cornyn:** Do you agree that on February 4 the letter that was written to Senator Grassley that um, with the allegation ATF sanctions or otherwise knowingly allowed the sale of assault weapons to a straw purchaser who then transferred them into Mexico is false. That letter dated February 4, 2011 is itself now false we now know.

> **Holder:** What I said is that it contains inaccurate information.

> **Cornyn:** Well, isn't that false?

> **Holder:** Well false, I don't want to quibble with you but false I think implies um, people, making a um, a decision to deceive and that was not what was going on there, people were in good faith giving what they thought was correct

information to Senator Grassley. We now know that information was not correct.

Cornyn: If you won't agree with me that it's false, it's not true, do you agree with that?

Holder: I'd say it's not accurate.[22]

Holder's "clarifications" failed to convince many members of Congress. By December 2011, ninety-one congressmen had signed a "no confidence" resolution against him;[23] by January 2012 that number had risen to 103.[24]

In late January 2012, the Justice Department released another raft of documents that further undermined Holder's testimony. The new emails indicated that Attorney General Holder's then Deputy Chief of Staff Monty Wilkinson had been alerted within hours of Brian Terry's death that guns found at the scene were linked to Operation Fast and Furious. The emails were leaked to National Public Radio, but even the generally liberal NPR could not put much of a gloss on this.

The exchanges, dated December 15, 2010, include an email from Dennis Burke to Wilkinson. Wilkinson was not some distant official in another part of the vast Justice Department—his job was to help oversee the work in Holder's personal office, and he was in frequent, direct contact with the attorney general.

Burke noted the death of Brian Terry in a message sent at 9:41 a.m.: "Not good. 18 miles w/in [U.S. territory]."

Less than half an hour later came Wilkinson's first reply: "Tragic. I've alerted the AG, the Acting DAG, Lisa, etc." An hour or so later,

Wilkinson asked Burke for follow-up information: "Please provide any additional details as they become available to you."

Later that evening Burke sent another email to Wilkinson with sobering news: "The guns found in the desert near the murder [sic] BP officer connect back to the investigation we were going to talk about—they were AK-47s purchased at a Phoenix gun store."

Wilkinson offered a short, quick reply: "I'll call tomorrow."[25]

The new emails again undercut Attorney General Holder, whose stance on the situation went from "I didn't know about the operation until a few weeks ago" to "I knew a year ago, but didn't know any details" to "my aide was informed of the details right after Brian Terry's death."

One thing Holder has been consistent on is refusing to accept any responsibility for Terry's death. In September 2011 he said, "The notion that [Fast and Furious] reaches into the upper levels of the Justice Department is something that at this point I don't think is supported by the facts and I think once we examine it and once the facts are revealed we'll see that's not the case."[26]

Appearing before the Senate Judiciary Committee in November 2011, Holder told Senator John Cornyn, "I have not apologized to [the Terry family], but I certainly regret what happened." Cornyn followed up, asking if Holder has "even talked to them." "I have not," Holder replied. "It pains me whenever there is the death of a law enforcement official, especially under the circumstances," Holder said. "It is not fair, however, to say the mistakes that happened in Fast and Furious directly led to the death of Agent Terry."[27]

This assertion was consistent with testimony Holder had given to Chairman Issa in May 2011 when he said, "The notion that somehow or other this Justice Department is responsible for those deaths that you mentioned, that assertion is offensive."[28]

In Holder's view, whoever was responsible for the deaths that occurred with guns given to Mexican drug cartels during Fast and Furious, it was certainly not the Justice Department under whose authority the ATF operation was run.

Testifying before a Senate committee in September 2011, Homeland Security Secretary Janet Napolitano denied knowing anything about Operation Fast and Furious until around the time of Brian Terry's murder. She told Senator Grassley during an October 2011 Senate Judiciary Committee hearing that she had not talked to her friend, former chief of staff, and former Arizona U.S. Attorney Dennis Burke about Fast and Furious. And in the same month, she told Congressman Jason Chaffetz, while appearing before the House Committee on Oversight and Government Reform, that she didn't believe she had ever spoken to Attorney General Holder about Fast and Furious.

Inside sources claim otherwise.

"When she says that [she] and Attorney General Eric Holder have not discussed it, that is a lie. That's why they keep asking her those questions in the Judicial, Oversight, Homeland Security Committee hearings. They've asked her that same question twice and she's lied twice," an inside source, who asked to remain anonymous, told me. "There are five emails linking her to Holder. They go back to two days after it happened—the first email was two days after Brian was killed."

The emails, the source says, show Holder discussing Brian Terry's murder with Napolitano.

"We honestly believe that Holder kept her in the dark about a lot of things, but we also know that her office approved the guns going across the border because CBP [Customs and Border Protection] agents had to go through her chain of command in order to let those guns go across the border," the source said. After all, hundreds of Fast and Furious guns were often transported by trucks and vans on major freeways, which have Border Patrol checkpoints going into Mexico.

If Holder in fact left Napolitano in the dark about the details of Fast and Furious, she still won't get out of the scandal without consequences. Perjury charges for lying to Congress could be on the table for the secretary.

"Oh she knew, she was briefed," an ATF source says. "There is no doubt about it. There was an ICE [Immigration and Customs Enforcement] Agent assigned specifically to be the co-case agent of Fast and Furious. He had to [file] an ICE report that either mirrored or referenced every ATF report that was done. The ICE Special Agent in Charge and ATF Special Agent in Charge and the ATF Assistant Special Agent in Charge, were constantly in battles over who gets 'this gun seizure or issue' to the point where I know phone calls were made to both headquarters to try and settle those disputes."[29]

"Let me tell you something about Janet," another inside source told me. "Janet will be lucky not to go to prison."

CHAPTER TEN

CONNECTING THE DOTS

"I have never heard an explanation from anyone involved in Operation Fast and Furious that I believe would justify what we did."

—ATF Agent John Dodson

While I was doing research for this book, I attended a fund-raiser for Border Patrol Agent Brian Terry's family—to help them defray legal expenses and to raise money so his mother Josephine could travel to congressional hearings—at the International Auto Museum in Scottsdale, Arizona. The room was filled with more than three hundred people as photos of Brian with family and friends flashed across a projector screen. A DJ played music in the background. Brian's mother and other members of the Terry family had flown from Michigan to be there. Family and close friends wore navy blue baseball style t-shirts printed with the words "Agent Terry" on the back. Arizona Governor Jan Brewer sat next to Josephine.

"The people of Arizona love you and will always remember Brian Terry," Brewer said. "Brian was a brave and faithful warrior."

Jay Dobyns was the evening's emcee. He acted as if he were hosting the Oscars. After each speaker, he returned to the stage with a new outfit and a ready supply of jokes. He toasted Brian's memory throughout the event, taking swigs from a large bottle of Jack Daniels. By the end of the fundraiser, the bottle was half full.

"I personally feel cheated I never got to meet him," Dobyns said. "This man dedicated his entire adult life to doing America's business."

Lana Domino, a close friend to Brian, shared her memories of him with the crowd. "He would give you the last dollar in his pocket and the shirt off his back," she said. "He loved his country as much as he loved his own family and friends."

Two managers from the ATF's Phoenix office showed up, though not ones who had directly overseen Fast and Furious. One of those agents was Tom Atteberry, who replaced Bill Newell as Special Agent in Charge (SAC) of the Phoenix Field Division, after Newell was whisked off to Washington, D.C., and promoted to special assistant to the assistant director of ATF's Office of Management.

Lingering beneath the warm tributes to the Border Patrol agent known to his friends and family as "Superman" was an underlying feeling of anger. You could sense it in the audience and see it in the eyes of Brian's family. The federal government still had not held accountable those who ordered the sale of high-powered weapons to Mexican drug cartels. Newell himself stood as a perfect example.

After the event, a few of the whistleblowers I'd gotten to know—Jay Dobyns, Vince Cefalu, and others—headed over to a popular dive bar (with a dirt parking lot and a wooden horse hitch out front) known as the Coach House, "Scottsdale's Oldest Tavern." Later, Tom Atteberry arrived. He seemed like a nice enough guy, if a little out of place. While the rest of us were in jeans and cowboy boots, Atteberry was dressed to the nines—suit, tie, and ATF lapel pin.

Atteberry chatted with a woman who had flown from Anchorage, Alaska, for the fundraiser for Terry's family. When she found out Atteberry had close ties to Chicago, she asked him what he thought of Andrew Traver, who had been Special Agent in Charge of the ATF's Chicago Field Division and was President Obama's nominee to become director of the ATF. Traver's nomination was controversial because he was a well-known opponent of gun ownership rights. The NRA's executive director for Legislative Action said of his nomination, "You might as well put an arsonist in charge of the fire department."[1] Traver's controversial gun control views had kept his nomination stalled in the Senate.

"He's a stand-up guy," Atteberry replied.

The woman asked Atteberry his views on the new long gun reporting measures being implemented through the Justice Department without the consent of Congress. The measures, announced by the Justice Department on July 8, 2011, targeted border state guns shops in California, Arizona, New Mexico, and Texas, requiring them to report the sale of multiple long gun rifles within a five-day period. According to the Justice Department:

> The international expansion and increased violence of transnational criminal networks pose a significant threat to the United States. Federal, state and foreign law enforcement agencies have determined that certain types of

semi-automatic rifles—greater than .22 caliber and with
the ability to accept a detachable magazine—are highly
sought after by dangerous drug trafficking organizations
and frequently recovered at violent crime scenes near the
Southwest Border.

This new reporting measure—tailored to focus only on
multiple sales of these types of rifles to the same person
within a five-day period—will improve the ability of the
Bureau of Alcohol, Tobacco, Firearms and Explosives to
detect and disrupt the illegal weapons trafficking networks
responsible for diverting firearms from lawful commerce to
criminals and criminal organizations. These targeted information requests will occur in Arizona, California, New Mexico, and Texas to help confront the problem of illegal gun
trafficking into Mexico and along the Southwest Border.[2]

The new reporting measure would not have helped prevent guns from
getting into the hands of cartel members during Fast and Furious, and
was just another version of Demand Letter 3. During that operation,
gun shop owners reported suspicious sales to ATF. It was ATF officials
themselves who told the shops to sell massive amounts of weapons to
straw purchasers working for Mexican drug cartels.

"They [gun dealers] were doing their job impeccably, to be honest
with you," Arizona Congressman Paul Gosar told me. "And that's what
I was trying to get at with the whole detail of our committee, is that
not only did they do their job, they did it impeccably. They called ATF,
they called these special field agents, they were doing their job—they
were uncomfortable. And they were doing it thoroughly. They were

almost forced, there were some that even said 'I'm not doing this, I have a right to say I'm not making any sales; as a business owner, I'm not'—some felt very uncomfortable and actually were forced into the hand of selling."[3]

In the eyes of Second Amendment defenders, the Obama Justice Department was punishing law-abiding gun shop owners for doing what they were told to do by federal officials. "Our headquarters completely set these [gun shop owners] up," an inside source told me.[4] The source also noted that after the joint press conference in Mexico City with President Obama in 2009, Mexican President Felipe Calderon traveled to New York City to obtain a lawyer. He had plans to sue American gun shops for crimes committed in Mexico.

In an interview with the Daily Caller, Congressman Issa accused the Justice Department of trying to divert attention from Fast and Furious through these new regulations. "It's disconcerting that Justice Department officials who may have known about or tried to cover up gunwalking in Operation Fast and Furious are continuing attempts to distract attention from clear wrongdoing."[5]

Senator Grassley responded in similar fashion:

> We've learned from our investigation of Fast and Furious that reporting multiple long gun sales would do nothing to stop the flow of firearms to known straw purchasers because many Federal Firearms Dealers are already voluntarily reporting suspicious transactions. In fact, in just the documents we've obtained, we are aware of 150 multiple long guns sales associated with the ATF's Fast and Furious case, and despite the fact that nearly all of these sales were

reported in real time by cooperating gun dealers, the ATF
watched the guns be transported from known straw purchasers to third parties and then let the guns walk away,
often across the border. This makes it pretty clear that the
problem isn't lack of burdensome reporting requirements.
The administration's continued overreach with regulations
continues, and is a distraction from its reckless policy to
allow guns to walk into Mexico.[6]

On August 3, 2011, the National Rifle Association sued the Justice
Department over its long gun reporting measures, arguing that department officials do not have the statutory authority to push through
new gun control measures without the consent of Congress. "They're
trying to bypass Congress, circumvent the law, usurp the authority of
Congress," said NRA Executive Vice President Wayne LaPierre in an
interview with Fox News.[7] J&G Sales, one of the Arizona gun dealers
used by ATF and the Department of Justice to run Operation Fast and
Furious, is represented by the NRA in the suit.

Attorney General Eric Holder told reporters during a press conference on August 3, 2010, "The measures that we are proposing are
appropriate ones to stop the flow of guns from the United States into
Mexico."[8]

Some argued that the Obama administration hoped to put gun
shop owners out of business—the ultimate in gun control—by over-
regulating them. "This is the argument that I've heard," a source inside
the ATF told me. The administration's attitude is: "So we can cripple
[gun shop owners] through regulations as well as financially and
achieve the same outcome as if we had passed laws."

With all this as backdrop, Tom Atteberry told the woman at the Coach House in Scottsdale that he thought the long gun reporting measures made "perfect sense."

As the new lead in Phoenix, Atteberry has to clean up a sizable mess. An affable man, he has been well received by most, if not all, of his subordinates. At the very least, they will give him a chance. But his demeanor and views that day left an impression that ATF was offering more of the same: another politicized leader eager to please those in power; the same kind of management that has plagued ATF for years, and led directly to the Fast and Furious scandal that even now has not unraveled fully. At the very least, Atteberry has been savvy enough to admit that Fast and Furious was not only a stupid operation, but in his opinion a criminal one.

The real question being asked by whistleblowers in Phoenix is whether corruption within ATF and the Justice Department will continue to be rewarded while those who attempt to expose it are punished and marginalized. As of February 2012, a year into the Fast and Furious investigation, there has not been a single firing of a senior management official involved in the program. That is troubling for the ATF whistleblowers who risked their careers to expose wrongdoing. It is an even more dismaying thought for all those who gathered to honor the memory of Brian Terry and raise money for his family.

The full consequences of Fast and Furious are not yet known. Emails released under congressional subpoena suggest that Attorney General Eric Holder and Homeland Security Secretary Janet Napolitano and their senior lieutenants were involved in devising and approving the program in 2009. Both Holder and Napolitano have made statements at odds with the facts. Holder has made statements at odds with his own testimony. As congressional investigators uncover more documents, what was initially a limited inquiry into one government program could become an investigation into perjury, obstruction of justice, and a government cover-up.

President Obama's connection to the scandal had yet to be thoroughly investigated, though there is ample evidence—indeed, public statements[9]—that one of his first priorities in office was to institute a program for tracing guns illegally trafficked into Mexico. Though there is no evidence yet that directly implicates Obama, the Fast and Furious scandal has all the hallmarks of major presidential scandals of the past, and the fact that so many leading players, from Janet Napolitano to Eric Holder, claimed ignorance of it is no defense, because even if their claims are true—and the evidence suggests otherwise—it is a stinging indictment of an irresponsible administration.

Officials, starting at ATF and going up into the White House, either knew about Operation Fast and Furious or should have known about it. The Fast and Furious operation was not a mere trifle, one of any number of small-consequence activities taking place throughout the federal government. This was a major operation taking place along an international border by an agency notorious for mismanagement. It was an operation in which lives could be lost if something went wrong, and an international incident could ensue. Improving America's relationship with Mexico was allegedly one of President Obama's foreign policy priorities; and from the beginning, Justice Department officials, including Attorney General Eric Holder, Secretary of State Hillary Clinton, and Homeland Security Secretary Janet Napolitano, stressed that the new effort to crack down on Mexican drug cartels with gun-tracing technology came directly from the president.

Fast and Furious is Barack Obama's Iran-Contra. Where President Reagan and his administration faced the legal consequences of a secret program to sell arms to Iran, President Obama must now face the legal consequences of his administration's secret program to sell arms to Mexican drug cartels. The weapons sold to Iran to fund anti-Communist guerillas in Nicaragua never, to anyone's knowledge, wound up killing U.S. citizens. Nevertheless, the mainstream press ran front-page stories on the scandal nearly every day for over a year. Under Obama, the same level of scrutiny has been absent.

Where the Reagan administration insisted on accountability, the Obama administration has moved to cover up its scandal. After congressional hearings and a presidential commission to investigate Iran-Contra, fourteen Reagan administration officials were indicted, including Secretary of Defense Caspar Weinberger, for perjury. And though President Reagan was not aware of, and certainly did not authorize, the operation, he nonetheless took full responsibility in a primetime address to the American people. "As angry as I may be about activities undertaken without my knowledge, I am still accountable for those activities," Reagan said. "As disappointed as I may be in some who served me, I'm still the one who must answer to the American people for this behavior."[10] It is difficult to imagine this coming from his successor, a president who has taken every opportunity to evade and shift blame.

As Congressman Issa noted,

> The administration has been trying to make [the Fast and Furious scandal] go away first by denying it, then by covering it up and delaying.... Very much like Iran-Contra and

other scandals of the past, the initial action [was] illegal, wrong, foolish, dangerous and ultimately deadly, which is bad enough. But the cover-up, the denial, giving Congress a letter flat saying "we don't let guns walk" when there was a program in which the emails show they called it gunwalking—they knew it was gunwalking and ultimately, Americans and Mexican citizens have paid with their lives.[11]

Some think that the Obama administration has tried to capitalize on a disaster. As Congressman Issa has said, "There is a 'Rahm Emanuel moment' that's pretty obvious," citing Emanuel's famous comment that "You never want a serious crisis to go to waste and what I mean by that is an opportunity to do things that you think you could not do before."[12]

Issa said, "When this disaster was happening, [the administration] decided to be opportunists and use it to expand the gun database that they are now executing by their own regulations in four states, and asking Congress to expand nationally. Very clearly, they made a crisis and they're using this crisis to somehow take away or limit people's Second Amendment rights."[13]

But there is a more insidious explanation too, and that is that Operation Fast and Furious was built to fail, from a straight law enforcement point of view, and built to succeed in promoting gun control. Certainly that has been its net effect, helping to justify the administration's new regulations on long guns. As Jay Dobyns told me, "Basically DOJ and the gun control advocates within DOJ and the Obama administration are saying, 'Hey look, go ahead and let these guns go. Violate your mission. Don't uphold the mission of your agency which is to combat violent crime and to protect the public, just go ahead and circumvent that because we're going to use you letting this type of activity take place to justify our arguments....' The sad thing for ATF is that they embrace that mentality and then they judged their success and they judged their effectiveness in making that happen by counting dead bodies. 'Well we have to have this long gun double check in place. We've got all these dead people here, see how tragic this is?' You killed them!"

"The ATF is supposed to be a guardian of our citizens," John Dodson said during congressional testimony. "ATF is supposed to be the sheepdog that protects against the wolves that prey upon our southern border. But rather than meet the wolf head on, we sharpened its teeth and added number to its claws, all the while we sat idly by watching, tracking, and noting as it became a more efficient killer."[14]

Why? What was the purpose of Fast and Furious? Was it really to "take down a major cartel"? If so, it certainly failed, and it is hard to see how it could have succeeded. While the guns walked during Fast and Furious could be traced to crime scenes (only after a crime, not before), there was never going to be any way to trace them to cartel kingpins. If the point was to gain evidence to arrest the straw buyers, they could have been arrested well before they walked guns across the border. Really the only thing Operation Fast and Furious could do was link American gun shop-sold guns to Mexican crimes—even if these sales were in fact forced by the ATF. Was Fast and Furious designed to help build a case for new gun control measures that could not otherwise pass Congress? Did the Obama administration and its political appointees put their zeal for their own political agenda ahead of public safety? The evidence suggests the answer is yes. Certainly there is evidence enough to suggest that, at a bare minimum, senior members of the Obama administration could face charges of perjury and obstruction of justice. For instance, we now know that:

- Eric Holder was sent five memos, personally addressed to him, in the summer of 2010 that detailed Operation Fast and Furious. He was briefed by his top aide Monty Wilkinson on Brian Terry's murder just hours after it happened in December 2010. Wilkinson knew on the day of the murder that it was linked to Fast and Furious and almost certainly informed his boss about that connection.

- Holder's testimony about what he knew and when he knew it has continually changed. In May 2011, he said he had known about the program for "a couple of weeks." In November 2011, Holder said he should have testified he had known about the program for a few months. He said the timeline of when he found out about Fast and Furious was a "distraction," and added that no one at the Justice Department had lied about the scandal. In February 2012, Holder claimed he first knew about the program in February 2011.

- Holder's closest associates knew about the gunwalking tactics used in the operation as early as April 2010. Holder's deputy attorney general for the Criminal Division, Lanny Breuer, approved wiretaps in the case and knew gunwalking tactics were being used. Former Arizona U.S. Attorney Dennis Burke, who served on Holder's Attorney General Advisory Committee while simultaneously overseeing the implementation of Fast and Furious in Phoenix, had regular interaction with Holder on border issues and policy. Yet Holder still claims he never heard about Fast and Furious prior to February 2011.

- White House officials, National Security Council senior directors Kevin O'Reilly and Greg Gatjanis[15] among them, were in contact with Bill Newell and the ATF Phoenix field office about Fast and Furious, and its overarching program Project Gunrunner, as early as July 2010.

- Homeland Security Secretary Janet Napolitano has feigned ignorance when questioned about Fast and Furious. She claims she only found out about the program after Brian Terry was murdered, although her close friend, former chief of staff, and special assistant Arizona U.S. Attorney Dennis Burke, agreed to all of the tactics being used in Fast and Furious. She visited the White House with Eric Holder to visit President Obama just a day before Holder testified on Capitol Hill about Fast and Furious, leaving the reason for her visit blank. Two of her agents were killed as a result of ATF gunwalking, yet she claims she never contacted the Justice Department to find out why they would allow such a reckless program to occur. She met with Holder to form a joint task force to investigate the murder of ICE agent Jaime Zapata, yet claims she has never even spoken to the attorney general about Fast and Furious.

- ATF whistleblowers suspect that when the Department of Justice inspector general finally issues her report, she will scold the ATF and its senior leadership and offer a full defense of Attorney General Holder and the other leaders of the Justice Department. The report will say Fast and Furious was a rogue operation run by rogue agents and will conclude that the ATF alone was ultimately responsible for the program. It will claim that ATF did not send enough information up the administrative chain to let supervisors within the Department of Justice know what exactly was transpiring. This is how the game is played. If President Obama is not going to punish his attorney general, then the inspector general isn't going to do it either.

It is difficult to argue anything other than that Attorney General Holder is a dangerously detached manager of the Department of Justice, or that he has lied to Congress and the public. Or both. Yet there has been no accountability for Fast and Furious—no one to step forward and say, "This was my fault. I take the blame." That, I think, is what bothers people the most. The families of Brian Terry and Jaime Zapata are still waiting for that moment, for someone to step forward and explain that his or her decision led to the deaths of their loved ones.

Even after the inspector general report is released, the stonewalling won't stop. As it stands now, the inspector general has access to 80,000 documents. Congress has only been given access to 6,000 of those documents, most of which are heavily redacted.

The only question now is whether Congressman Issa and his allies on Capitol Hill will be persistent enough and determined enough to find the evidence needed to expose wrongdoing at the top. Practically no one with knowledge of the operation in Phoenix believes that Justice Department and Homeland Security leaders in Washington were kept in the dark about Fast and Furious. The real issue is whether the congressional investigators can find someone who will talk. Will anybody involved in Fast and Furious face consequences for breaking U.S. and international law and contributing to the deaths of hundreds of people? Are criminal charges ever going to be on their way?

For those who have seen the brutality of Mexico's drug cartels up close—those who could conceivably be their next victims—the lack of accountability in the Obama administration is troubling. Arizona Sheriff Paul Babeu has gone so far as to say that those involved in the scandal are accessories to murder. "What I learned just as a regular police officer is that anybody who is involved in assisting other people in crimes are called accomplices," he says. "And they're charged as well with the same crimes as the people who pulled the trigger."

Will men like Bill Newell be prosecuted for illegally trafficking weapons into Mexico, trafficking weapons to ruthless drug cartels? By his own standards, he should be held accountable. After all he did say, "[Those who arm cartels] have as much blood on their hands as the criminals that use them."

As former Congressman Jim Lightfoot puts it, "It's time to treat the disease, not the symptoms." Lightfoot had come to the ATF's rescue when congressional Republicans wanted to shut down the bureau in the wake of the botched 1993 raid on the Branch Davidian compound in Waco. Lightfoot convinced them that with reforms and new management the bureau could overcome its problems of politicization and negligence. Now Lightfoot is not so sure he was right.

As shocking as this scenario is, it suits the known facts. Under Eric Holder, the ATF was deputized to change the nation's gun laws by putting in place a shadowy operation designed to prove a falsehood: that weapons sold by U.S. gun shops, especially "assault weapons," are the cause of Mexico's drug violence. By creating public outrage, President Obama, Eric Holder, and other administration officials, all with longstanding records of hostility against the Second Amendment, hoped to reinstate the assault weapons ban, which had been one of their early, but failed, political goals. Eric Holder admitted in February 2012 the reimplementation of the assault rifle ban is still a policy stance of the Obama administration.

"This administration has consistently favored the reinstitution of the assault weapons ban. It is something that we think was useful in the past with regard to the reduction that we've seen in crime, and certainly would have a positive impact on our relationship and the crime situation in Mexico."[16]

These are the facts: There are still 1,400 Fast and Furious guns missing, and ATF agents are not actively trying to track them down. Ten thousand rounds of ammunition were sold to cartel-linked straw buyers under the watch of the ATF. Eight hundred of the original 2,500 weapons sold through Fast and Furious have already been linked to criminal activity. We can be certain that is only the beginning. We'll be seeing the lethal consequences of this program for years to come, and many lives will be taken in cold blood along the way. Even Eric Holder admits as much. "It's going to continue to have tragic consequences," he told congressional investigators.[17]

■ ■ ■ ■ ■

The lethal and devastating consequences of Fast and Furious are clear. It is also clear that the administration is attempting to use those consequences to restrict gun rights. That raises the question: If given another four years, how might the Obama administration pursue its anti-gun agenda? Unless Republicans and pro-Second Amendment Democrats are routed in congressional races in 2012, it is highly unlikely the Obama administration will have a legislature willing to pass gun control legislation. Support for gun rights in America is as strong as ever. The NRA boasts 4 million members. Self-reported gun ownership in the United States is at its highest point since 1993. One in three Americans personally own a gun.[18] According to Gallup polls, support for new gun laws, regulations, and the reinstatement of the assault rifle ban is at an all time low.[19] Still, Obama has demonstrated that he doesn't need Congress to enact his agenda. He can try to impose it through executive orders, or possibly with a newly configured Supreme Court, or with the help of United Nations bureaucrats.

So far, President Obama has appointed two justices to the Supreme Court—Elena Kagan and Sonia Sotomayor—both of whom are on record as opposing individual gun rights. Kagan drafted a Clinton-era executive order that would outlaw certain high-powered rifles,[20] and as a law clerk to Justice Thurgood Marshall she wrote memos denouncing Second Amendment rights.[21] Sonia Sotomayor has argued, as a Supreme Court justice, that the Second Amendment should be seen as a collective, not an individual right,[22] and that local governments have the authority to limit gun ownership.[23]

Recent landmark gun rights decisions such as *District of Columbia v. Heller*, which upheld gun rights within the District of Columbia, and *McDonald v. Chicago*, which upheld the Second Amendment as applicable to state law, were decided by 5-to-4 votes. Justices Antonin Scalia and Anthony Kennedy, who voted with the majority, are both pushing eighty. In a second term, Obama might have the opportunity to replace one or both of them with a justice who is hostile to individual gun rights. But the Supreme Court isn't the only place Obama can do damage to the Second Amendment. Federal court appointments give Obama the perfect opportunity to stack benches around the country with anti-gun ideologues. In December 2011, Senate Republicans actually filibustered to prevent the appointment of Obama's D.C. federal appeals court nominee Caitlin Halligan because of her extreme anti-Second Amendment views.[24] Even if stymied there, President Obama has the power to appoint U.S. attorneys who can push his anti-gun agenda.

NRA Executive Vice President Wayne LaPierre believes the Obama administration is purposefully keeping gun owners in the dark about its future plans, should the president be re-elected. "Obama administration officials know that it's good politics to avoid making gun control a public issue," he says. "They hope that they can lull gun owners into a false sense of security and then play us for fools in the 2012 election."[25]

Barack Obama is also content to let unelected bureaucrats at the United Nations dictate America's gun laws. His administration has supported the United Nations Arms Trade Treaty (ATT). The alleged purpose of the treaty is to prevent crime, terrorism, and even war by regulating the sale of guns, but it is a rarely noted irony that some of the biggest supporters of the treaty are also the world's most brazen supporters of terrorism, such as Iran, Syria, and Cuba. Its proposed regulations extend to the level of firearms accessories, including scopes and magazines. Secretary of State Hillary Clinton expressed her support for the treaty in October 2009, saying, "The United States is prepared to work hard for a strong international standard in this area by seizing the opportunity presented by the Conference on the Arms Trade Treaty at the United Nations....The United States is committed to actively pursuing a strong and robust treaty that contains the highest possible, legally binding standards for the international transfer of conventional weapons. We look forward to this negotiation."[26]

The final draft of the treaty is scheduled to be completed by summer 2012. The State Department, Department of Justice, and ATF have taken a leadership role in pushing the treaty.[27] The Bush administration refused to participate in the negotiations, but the Obama administration has been a willing participant in drafting the treaty, with Secretary of State Hillary Clinton at the helm. Obama has said he would like to see the treaty ratified as a way of demonstrating America's respect for "international norms."

Because the UN's definition of "criminal activity" in the treaty is so broad, American gun owners could find themselves prosecuted if UN officials deemed owning some firearms a crime. If the treaty were to be effective, it would imply the necessity for strict regulation of individual firearms ownership.[28] Mexico wants the treaty to regulate hunting rifles, because it claims hunting rifles are used by drug cartels. But of course any weapon that can be used for sport or self-defense could also be used in ways that the treaty might regulate.[29]

The treaty calls for international reporting measures that would require countries to trace and keep track of weapons sold and transferred. Not only would this consume a massive amount of government resources, it would also be intrusive. Many Second Amendment advocates regard the creation of a nationwide database of lawful gun owners and a catalog of every firearm they own as an ominous expansion of government power. The most vocal supporters of the treaty in the United States are gun control organizations such as the Brady Campaign and the Joyce Foundation (the anti-gun organization that once counted Obama as a member).

■ ■ ■ ■ ■

Would a second term bring us another Operation Fast and Furious? All one can say for certain is that the administration seems to feel little remorse for the first one. In his 2013 budget, President Obama deliberately stripped language that would prevent another Fast and Furious from happening, saying the language was "not necessary."[30] The slights to the Terry family by key figures in the Fast and Furious scandal defy explanation. Attorney General Holder, for example, took nearly a year to offer condolences directly to the family; and when he did so, in a form email letter, it was only after prodding by numerous members of Congress—and Holder's associates leaked it to the media first.

Shortly before his resignation as U.S. attorney, Dennis Burke denied the family a routine request for "crime victim" status in the case against Jaime Avila, which would have allowed the family to talk with prosecutors on the case and testify at Mr. Avila's sentencing hearing. Burke argued that the Terry family was not "directly or proximately harmed" by Jaime Avila's purchase of the gun that was used to kill Brian in December 2010—a line echoed by Attorney General Holder.

A former Florida U.S. attorney took issue with the claim. "The government apparently is saying they're not victims, even though it is a federal crime that put the murder weapon in the hand of the killer of Brian Terry," Kendall Coffey charged. "They are simply rights of respect, rights of communication and the right to be heard."[31]

The Terry family has yet to receive a full explanation of Brian's death. They still lack an incident report that describes the evidence at his murder scene and the circumstances surrounding the crime.

Once Dennis Burke resigned, the Terry case was transferred out of the Arizona U.S. Attorney's Office to San Diego, where it was immediately sealed from the public by a federal judge, preventing the media and the Terry family from seeing any of the information in the case, including testimony, court arguments, briefings and evidence. The files remain sealed as of this writing. Almost comically, the reasons for sealing the file were also sealed.

Despite the extreme secrecy surrounding the murder, some additional information has become known. This has only raised more questions. Although published reporters indicated at the time of Brian Terry's death that two guns had been found at the scene—both of which were traced to Fast and Furious—there is evidence that there might have been a third gun.

During Brian Terry's funeral, Border Patrol agents, who have since been issued gag orders, were overheard discussing the discovery of three weapons at the scene.[32] An email sent less than twelve hours after Terry's death, which was later obtained by investigators, discussed ballistics tracing for two AK-47s, but also mentioned a third gun that was in the process of being traced by the FBI.

"I initiated an urgent firearms trace request on both of the firearms and then contacted the NTC [National Tracing Center] to ensure the traces were conducted today," the email said. Another stated the firearms "recovered earlier today by the FBI" were being traced.[33] Phoenix Special Assistant in Charge George Gillett responded, "Are those two in addition to the gun already recovered this morning?"[34] A March 2011 audio recording made by Andre Howard, owner of Lone Wolf Trading Company, as he was speaking to ATF's Hope MacAllister also referenced a third gun. One of Howard's recordings revealed the following exchange in reference to Brian Terry's shooting:

MacAllister: Well there was two.

Howard: There's three weapons.

MacAllister: There's three weapons.

Howard: I know that.

MacAllister: And yes, there's serial numbers for all three.

Howard: That's correct.

The Justice Department and the FBI have flatly denied the existence of a third weapon in Brian Terry's death. "The FBI has made clear that reports of a third gun recovered from the perpetrators at the scene of Agent Terry's murder are false," the Department claimed in an October 17 report.[35]

So what is the real story? Why does it matter how many guns were at the scene—and why would the Department of Justice want to deny the existence of a third gun with such certitude? To observers of the case, there is only one explanation.

The investigation of Fast and Furious has revealed that at least six FBI informants were used during the operation, as well as an undetermined number who work with the Drug Enforcement Administration. These informants, especially those working to infiltrate Mexican drug cartels, have a long and checkered history. Some have been described as "cold-blooded killers" who have seen their relationships with the federal government severed. Some, but not all.

Some congressional investigators believe the evidence suggests that the ATF's Hope MacAllister was working with a confidential FBI informant on the Fast and Furious operation. She would tell the informant which weapons to buy at area gun stores and then tell owners like Andre Howard exactly how many weapons certain straw purchasers would be requesting in advance of the orders being placed.

"At least one individual who is allegedly an FBI informant might have been in communication with, and was perhaps even conspiring with, at least one suspect whom ATF was monitoring," Grassley and Issa wrote in a joint letter to FBI director Robert Mueller.

A separate confidential source has told me that the reason the FBI hid the third gun from evidence was because "it was linked to their confidential informant, or his brother."

If this is true, the conclusion would offer another shattering blow to the family of Brian Terry, the young man who served his country in the United States military and then on the dangerous Mexican border. Not only might he have been killed with guns provided by the U.S. government—the federal government might also have paid, rewarded, and then protected the man who pulled the trigger.

■ ■ ■ ■ ■

In the end, Operation Fast and Furious wasn't a "botched" program. It was a calculated and lethal decision to purposely place thousands of guns into the hands of ruthless criminals. The guns weren't accidentally misplaced or lost. They didn't somehow "fall into the wrong hands" by mistake. The operation was a coordinated and planned effort not to track guns, but to arm thugs south of the border for political gain.

"Justice has blood on their hands," Issa has said. "What we do know is that enough weapons were down there that inevitably more will die, both Americans and Mexicans. And this program is the kind of program that will continue unless we get a change in how Justice views things, and certainly a change in how political appointees are viewing it." That work continues.

APPENDICES

APPENDIX 1

TIMELINE

April 2009: Obama calls for Holder to re-evaluate all gun trafficking policies with Mexico. Eric Holder, Barack Obama, and Hillary Clinton claim 90 percent of guns in Mexico come from the United States.

May 2009: Southwest Border Initiative is launched, new ATF agents and teams sent to border, money is allocated from the stimulus to fund continue "Project Gunrunner."

September 2009: Fast and Furious launched.

December 2009: ATF Special Agent John Dodson transferred to Phoenix, starts questioning tactics of Fast and Furious.

January 2010: Murder rate in Mexico skyrockets.

March/April 2010: Top ATF officials from Washington, D.C., including ATF Acting Director Kenneth Melson, visit Phoenix Field Division.

July 2010: ATF agents working in Mexico find out about Fast and Furious, ask for it to be stopped, and are told by Phoenix Field Division that it will stop (but the operation continues until December 2010).

October 2010: Dodson transferred away from ATF and Fast and Furious to the FBI.

December 14–15, 2010: Border Patrol Agent Brian Terry is killed on duty.

December 15, 2010: Gun used to kill Terry is traced back to straw purchaser Jaime Avila, who bought the gun at Lone Wolf Trading Company. The gun was sold as part of Fast and Furious.

December 15, 2010: *Washington Post* publishes a hit piece on border gun shop owners, accusing them of selling to cartels and fueling violence in Mexico.

December 15, 2010: Panic sets in. Emails fly in DOJ and ATF about the connection between Fast and Furious and the Terry murder.

December 21, 2010: Napolitano attends funeral of Brian Terry in Michigan.

Early January 2011: John Dodson speaks to Senator Charles Grassley about Fast and Furious. Investigation from the Senate Judiciary Committee begins.

January 20, 2011: ATF Special Agent in Charge Bill Newell holds press conference indicting straw purchasers. He says that those who purchased guns for the criminals who used them to kill are just as guilty for the crimes committed with them. Asked about gunwalking, Newell says, "Hell no"—we didn't let guns walk.

January 27 and 30, 2011: Grassley sends letter to Assistant Attorney General Lanny Breuer asking for details about Fast and Furious, citing claims by Dodson that guns were walking.

Between January and February 2011: Emails between Arizona U.S. Attorney's Office and the DOJ in D.C. show U.S. Attorney Dennis Burke saying they should deny everything Dodson said.

February 4, 2011: Breuer sends response to Grassley, claiming everything Dodson said was false.

February 15, 2011: ICE Agent Jaime Zapata killed in Mexico.

February 23, 2011: CBS News issues a report full of unnamed sources about Fast and Furious.

March 2011: Grassley hands investigation over to House Oversight Committee Chairman Darrell Issa because Issa has subpoena power.

March 3, 2011: Whistleblower John Dodson goes on national television with CBS News' Sharyl Attkisson and gives the details of Fast and Furious.

March 27, 2011: Obama is asked about Fast and Furious on Univision, and denies that he or Holder knew.

April 2011: Issa starts digging into what Eric Holder knew about Fast and Furious. Subpoenas are issued and ignored.

May 2, 2011: Attorney General Eric Holder and Department of Homeland Security Secretary Janet Napolitano visit the White House.

May 3, 2011: Holder testifies before the House Judiciary Committee, Issa grills him on when he knew about Fast and Furious. Holder says, "In the past few weeks."

June 2011: DOJ sends Issa's office 800 pages of redacted material, described as "black" paper. Issa threatens to hold Obama admininstration in contempt for stonewalling.

June 15, 2011: First full-blown House Oversight Committee hearing held on Fast and Furious with whistleblowers, DOJ Assistant Attorney General Ronald Weich, and Senator Grassley. Democrats call for gun control as a result of Fast and Furious.

June 30, 2011: House Democrats submit gun control legislation.

July 11, 2011: Deputy Attorney General James Cole issues new long gun reporting measures through a DOJ regulation, forcing border state gun shops to report multiple sales of long gun rifles in a three-day period. (Also known as "demand letter 3.")

July 14, 2011: Emails surface showing Fast and Furious was designed to promote gun control.

July 26, 2011: Second full blown House Oversight Committee Hearing featuring ATF agents working in Mexico who were never told about Fast and Furious. ATF management officials from the Phoenix Field Office testify, Newell admits the White House was involved in Fast and Furious but denies ever letting guns walk.

August 16, 2011: ATF management agents responsible for Fast and Furious are promoted.

August 30, 2011: Acting ATF Director Kenneth Melson reassigned, new acting director appointed.

August 31, 2011: U.S. Attorney for Arizona Dennis Burke resigns, makes no mention of Fast and Furious in resignation letter, gives his office a glowing recommendation.

September 2011: Issa starts asking about a third Fast and Furious gun left at Terry murder scene taken from evidence.

September 6, 2011: Brian Terry federal case moved from Arizona to San Diego in order to avoid conflict of interest.

October 3, 2011: Memos surface detailing Fast and Furious, addressed directly to Eric Holder, dated July and August 2010, nearly a full year before he admitted knowing about the program to Congress.

October 6, 2011: Representative Raul Labrador becomes first member of Congress to call for Holder's resignation.

October 7, 2011: Holder sends letter to Congress, still denying he knew the tactics being used, or about Fast and Furious, and insisting that he was "consistent and accurate" in his May 3 testimony about his knowledge of the program.

November 1, 2011: Assistant Attorney General Lanny Breuer admits in sworn testimony he knew gunwalking was happening as far back as 2010, but "forgot" to inform Holder, making the letter sent to Congress from his office in February 2011 totally false. Two more guns linked to Fast and Furious found by Pinal County Sheriff's office during raid of Sinaloa cartel.

November 8, 2011: Holder testifies before Senate Judiciary Committee, refuses to apologize to Terry family, says it is not fair to link Terry's death to Fast and Furious, and insists the focus on when he knew about Fast and Furious is a "distraction." Holder also says he hasn't talked to Napolitano about Fast and Furious. Holder admits for the first time that gunwalking occurred. Later that week, Holder finally sends Terry family an email apology, after leaking it to the press first.

November 12, 2011: Brian Terry federal case file sealed by judge. Reason judge sealed the case is also sealed.

November 14, 2011: Fundraiser held for Brian Terry's mother, Josephine, in Scottsdale, Arizona.

December 7, 2011: Senator Grassley calls for Breuer's resignation on the Senate floor.

December 8, 2011: Representative Sensenbrenner brings up impeachment of Holder for Fast and Furious investigation stonewalling. Breuer letter withdrawn because it was so full of lies.

December 15, 2011: One-year anniversary of Brian Terry's murder. Fast and Furious comes up in GOP primary debate for first time.

February 2, 2012: Eric Holder testifies before the House Judiciary Committee and claims the Department of Justice is in no way involved in a coverup.

APPENDIX 2

```
From:              Burke, Dennis (USAAZ)
To:
Sent:              12/15/2010 9:09:23 AM
Subject:           Re: INITIAL TELEPHONIC - SHOT FIRED - Nogales, AZ


Horrible.


From:              ████████  (HQ) [RC-1 ████████████]
Sent: Wednesday, December 15, 2010 03:31 AM
To: Burke, Dennis (USAAZ)
Subject: Fw: INITIAL TELEPHONIC - SHOT FIRED - Nogales, AZ

Our agent has passed away.


From: ████████████
To: OIOC-SIT SHOTS FIRED INJURY-DEATH
Cc: SITROOM
Sent: Wed Dec 15 02:31:32 2010
Subject: INITIAL TELEPHONIC - SHOT FIRED - Nogales, AZ

INITIAL TELEPHONIC

On December 14, 2010, a BORTAC agent working in the Nogales, AZ AOR was shot. The agent was conducting Border Patrol
operations 18 miles north of the international boundary when he encountered RC-5 ████████ unidentified subjects. Shots were
exchanged resulting in the agent being shot. At this time, the agent is being transported to an area where he can be air lifted to
an emergency medical center. RC-5 ████████████████████

Updates to follow.
```

Then Arizona U.S. Attorney Dennis Burke received an email—most likely from the Border Patrol—alerting him that Border Patrol Agent Brian Terry had been killed. Earlier Burke had received a message about a shooting incident near the border.

APPENDIX 3

From:	Wilkinson, Monty (OAG) (SMO)
To:	Burke, Dennis (USAAZ)
Sent:	12/15/2010 10:04:52 AM
Subject:	RE: INITIAL TELEPHONIC - SHOT FIRED - Nogales, AZ

Tragic. I've alerted the AG, the Acting DAG, Lisa, etc.

From: Burke, Dennis (USAAZ)
Sent: Wednesday, December 15, 2010 9:41 AM
To: Wilkinson, Monty (OAG)
Subject: Fw: INITIAL TELEPHONIC - SHOT FIRED - Nogales, AZ

Not good.

18 miles w/in.

From: ████████████ (HQ) [RC-1 ████████████]
Sent: Wednesday, December 15, 2010 03:31 AM
To: Burke, Dennis (USAAZ)
Subject: Fw: INITIAL TELEPHONIC - SHOT FIRED - Nogales, AZ

Our agent has passed away.

From: ████
To: OIOC-SIT SHOTS FIRED INJURY-DEATH
Cc: SITROOM
Sent: Wed Dec 15 02:31:32 2010
Subject: INITIAL TELEPHONIC - SHOT FIRED - Nogales, AZ

INITIAL TELEPHONIC

On December 14, 2010, a BORTAC agent working in the Nogales, AZ AOR was shot. The agent was conducting Border Patrol operations 18 miles north of the International boundary when he encountered RC-5 ████████ unidentified subjects. Shots were exchanged resulting in the agent being shot. At this time, the agent is being transported to an area where he can be air lifted to an emergency medical center. RC-5 ████████████████

Updates to follow.

December 15, 2010, email chain regarding Border Patrol Agent Brian Terry's death. A redacted sender alerted then U.S. Attorney Dennis Burke to Terry's having been shot, and one hour later emailed that Terry had died. Burke forwarded the email message to Eric Holder's then Deputy Chief of Staff Monty Wilkinson. Wilkinson acknowledged the email and wrote that he had alerted Attorney General Eric Holder.

APPENDIX 4

From: Wilkinson, Monty (OAG) (SMO)
To: Burke, Dennis (USAAZ)
Sent: 12/15/2010 11:15:51 AM
Subject: RE: INITIAL TELEPHONIC - SHOT FIRED - Nogales, AZ

Please provide any additional details as they become available to you.

Thanks,

Monty

From: Burke, Dennis (USAAZ)
Sent: Wednesday, December 15, 2010 9:41 AM
To: Wilkinson, Monty (OAG)
Subject: Fw: INITIAL TELEPHONIC - SHOT FIRED - Nogales, AZ

Not good.

18 miles w/in.

From: ▮▮▮▮▮▮▮ (HQ) [RC-1 ▮▮▮▮▮▮▮]
Sent: Wednesday, December 15, 2010 03:31 AM
To: Burke, Dennis (USAAZ)
Subject: Fw: INITIAL TELEPHONIC - SHOT FIRED - Nogales, AZ

Our agent has passed away.

From: ▮▮▮▮▮▮▮
To: OIOC-SIT SHOTS FIRED INJURY-DEATH
Cc: SITROOM
Sent: Wed Dec 15 02:31:32 2010
Subject: INITIAL TELEPHONIC - SHOT FIRED - Nogales, AZ

INITIAL TELEPHONIC

On December 14, 2010, a BORTAC agent working in the Nogales, AZ AOR was shot. The agent was conducting Border Patrol operations 18 miles north of the international boundary when he encountered [RC-5 ▮▮▮▮] unidentified subjects. Shots were exchanged resulting in the agent being shot. At this time, the agent is being transported to an area where he can be air lifted to an emergency medical center. [RC-5 ▮▮▮▮▮▮▮▮▮▮▮▮▮▮▮▮▮▮▮▮▮▮▮▮▮]

Updates to follow.

After alerting Eric Holder to Brian Terry's death, Monty Wilkinson sent Dennis Burke a follow-up email, asking for "any additional details as they become available." Later that day, Dennis Burke informed Wilkinson that the guns found at the murder scene were linked back to a case he planned to discuss with Wilkinson.

APPENDIX 5

Thanks, Dennis. Terrible situation.

From: Burke, Dennis (USAAZ)
Sent: Wednesday, December 15, 2010 1:21 PM
To: Wilkinson, Monty (OAG)
Subject: Fw: Incident involving the Bortac Agent this morning

---

From: ███████ (USAAZ) 3
Sent: Wednesday, December 15, 2010 11:45 AM
To: Hernandez, Rachel (USAAZ); ███████ (USAAZ); Scheel, Ann (USAAZ); USAAZ-TUCADMIN; USAAZ-TUCAFU; USAAZ-TUCAUSA; USAAZ-TUCFLU; USAAZ-TUCLawclerks; USAAZ-TUCPARA; USAAZ-TUCSAUSA; USAAZ-TUCSECY; USAAZ-TUCStudents; USAAZ-TUCSupport; USAAZ-TUCVW
Subject: Incident involving the Bortac Agent this morning

Deputy Chief ███████████ provided the following information regarding the incident this morning that resulted in the death of an agent.

All Tucson Sector Employees,

It is with a heavy heart that I inform you of the death of Border Patrol Agent Brian A. Terry who was shot and killed during an encounter with armed subjects. Agent Terry was working in the "Peck Well" area near Rio Rico, Arizona when he was fatally injured.

During the encounter, one assailant was wounded and immediately taken into custody. Three additional suspects were apprehended shortly thereafter. Border Patrol agents are currently tracking a fifth suspect and I assure you that every effort will be expended to bring this remaining suspect into custody.

Agent Terry entered on duty with Academy Class 699 on July 23, 2007. He is survived by his parents and sister in Detroit, Michigan. Please keep Agent Terry and his family in your thoughts and prayers as they have made the ultimate sacrifice in service to our country.

This is a stark reminder of the realities we face in our mission to protect our borders and our communities. We will continue to stand firm in our commitment to that mission.

In difficult times like these it is important that we turn to and support one another. Peer Support members, the Tucson Sector Chaplaincy Program, and the Employee Assistance Program are all available to any employee who may need them. Updates will be provided about this tragic situation as soon as information becomes available.

███████will be the lead AUSA on any prosecution and is in contact with the investigators. Please forward any inquiries you receive to ██████

A staffer with the Arizona United States Attorney's Office sent an email to all employees informing them of Brian Terry's murder. The email indicates the Arizona U.S. Attorney's Office had plans to prosecute those responsible.

APPENDIX 6

I certainly appreciate the promotion to 'Agent' but alas, I'm merely a press flack for Secy. Napolitano. Final details are being formulated, I am looping in Melanie Roe from CBP who can provide further guidance shortly.

.anks,

Matt

Matt Chandler
Deputy Press Secretary
Office of Public Affairs
U.S. Department of Homeland Security
O - (202) RC-1
C - (202)
RC-1

From: Clemens, Shelley (USAAZ) RC-1
Sent: Wednesday, December 15, 2010 6:00 PM
To: Chandler, Matthew (DHS)
Subject: FW: FBI/CBP Presser

Agent Chandler,

I have been notified by USA Dennis Burke of this press conference. I will be there to represent the US Attorney's Office. Where will it be held at?
Thanks
elley

From: Chandler, Matthew (DHS)
Sent: Wednesday, December 15, 2010 3:30 PM
To: Burke, Dennis (USAAZ)
Subject: FBI/CBP Presser

CBP is calling FBI now, they're going to aim for 5 PM ish in Tucson. We'd love to have someone from the USAO there...no chance you could make it down? Vow to prosecute to the full extent, etc?

Homeland Security Deputy Press Secretary Matt Chandler set up a press conference with the Arizona U.S. Attorney's Office, suggesting that the U.S. Attorney pledge to prosecute to the full extent of the law Terry's killers.

APPENDIX 7

From:	Wilkinson, Monty (OAG) (SMO)	
To:	Burke, Dennis (USAAZ)	
Sent:	12/15/2010 7:27:01 PM	
Subject:	Re: FBI/CBP Presser	

I'll call tomorrow.

From: Burke, Dennis (USAAZ)
To: Wilkinson, Monty (OAG)
Sent: Wed Dec 15 19:22:26 2010
Subject: FW: FBI/CBP Presser

The guns found in the desert near the murder BP officer connect back to the investigation we were going to talk about – they were AK-47s purchased at a Phoenix gun store.

From: ███████████ (USAAZ)
Sent: Wednesday, December 15, 2010 5:19 PM
To: Burke, Dennis (USAAZ); Scheel, Ann (USAAZ)
Subject: Fw: FBI/CBP Presser

BP decided to make a statement and not allow questions. RC-5 ██████████████████████ Based on that, we chose not to make a formal statement, RC-6 ████████████████
RC-6 ██████████████████████████████ They referenced that ████ and I were there for the USAO and to support their office.

████████ was here and advised that the 2 guns are tied to an on-going Phoenix ATF inv. You will probably get a call from Bill Newell.
████████

Dennis Burke informed Monty Wilkinson that the guns found at Terry's murder scene were purchased at a Phoenix area gun store and were tied to an investigation Burke planned on discussing with Wilkinson.

APPENDIX 8

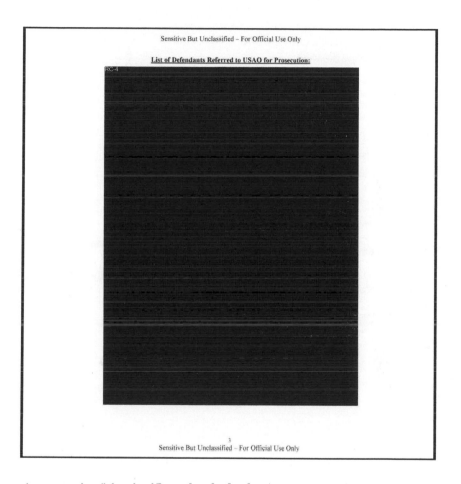

An example of the significant level of redaction on many documents given to the House Oversight Committee from the Justice Department about Operation Fast and Furious.

APPENDIX 9

RC-1

om: Scheel, Ann (USAAZ)
nt: Wednesday, December 15, 2010 7:24 PM
.o: Burke, Dennis (USAAZ); Clemens, Shelley (USAAZ)
Subject: Re: FBI/CBP Presser

Wow! Timely.

From: Burke, Dennis (USAAZ)
Sent: Wednesday, December 15, 2010 07:21 PM
To: Clemens, Shelley (USAAZ); Scheel, Ann (USAAZ)
Subject: RE: FBI/CBP Presser

Thanks. I just talked to Bill Newell about it.   The guns tie back to Emory's Fast and Furious case.

From: Clemens, Shelley (USAAZ)
Sent: Wednesday, December 15, 2010 5:19 PM
To: Burke, Dennis (USAAZ); Scheel, Ann (USAAZ)
Subject: Fw: FBI/CBP Presser

BP decided to make a statement and not allow questions. RC-5   Based on
that, we chose not to make a formal statement RC-5
RC-5   They referenced that John and I were there for the USAO and to support their
fice.

Nate Grey was here and advised that the 2 guns are tied to an on-going Phoenix ATF inv. You will probably get a call
from Bill Newell.
Shelley

From: Chandler, Matthew (DHS)
Sent: Wednesday, December 15, 2010 06:12 PM
To: Clemens, Shelley (USAAZ); ROE, MELANIE N. <RC-1   dhs.gov>
Subject: RE: FBI/CBP Presser

No worries at all. We really appreciate your support and assistance with this.

From: Clemens, Shelley (USAAZ) RC-1
Sent: Wednesday, December 15, 2010 6:11 PM
To: Chandler, Matthew (DHS); ROE, MELANIE N.
Subject: RE: FBI/CBP Presser

Sorry for the faux pas. I spoke with Agent Cantu, and was told 5:00 at Sector Headquarters on Swan.

From: Chandler, Matthew (DHS)
Sent: Wednesday, December 15, 2010 4:09 PM
o: Clemens, Shelley (USAAZ); ROE, MELANIE N.
Subject: RE: FBI/CBP Presser

Hi Shelley –

Emails between then Assistant U.S. Attorney Ann Scheel and U.S. Attorney Dennis Burke show extensive discussion about Fast and Furious guns being found at the scene of Border Patrol Agent Brian Terry's murder less than twenty-four hours after he was killed.

APPENDIX 10

Note: Two pages have been withheld from this seven page document because they included sensitive investigative details and information about targets/subjects.

A flippant title for a deadly operation, "Fast and Furious" took its name from a bad Hollywood movie.

APPENDIX 11

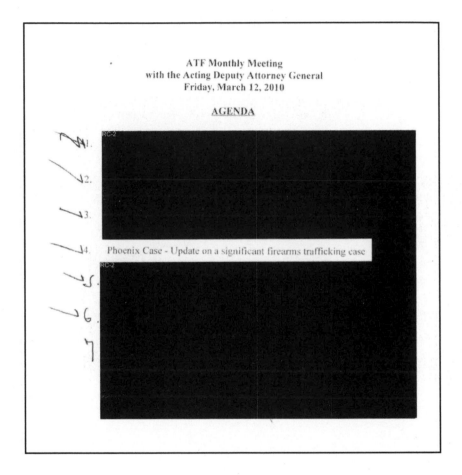

Another example of the significant level of redaction on many documents given to the House Oversight Committee from the Justice Department about Operation Fast and Furious. This is the agenda for a monthly ATF meeting held on March 12, 2010, and attended by high level Justice Department officials, including Eric Holder's lieutenant Gary Grindler. Grindler took extensive notes about Operation Fast and Furious during this meeting.

APPENDIX 12

Attorney General Holder's then lieutenant Gary Grindler attended a monthly meeting with the ATF on March 12, 2010, where he scrawled these notes about a long gun reporting measure and multiple long rifle sale issues. Grindler now serves as Holder's chief of staff.

APPENDIX 13

A photo of semi-automatic rifles shows Gary Grindler's handwriting. "No multiple sales reporting rifles, need req. long rifles," he wrote.

APPENDIX 14

```
From:          Chait, Mark R.
Sent:          Wednesday, July 14, 2010 10:25 AM
To:            Newell, William D.
Cc:            McMahon, William G.
Subject:       Re: SIR


Bill - can you see if these guns were all purchased from same FfL and
at one time. We are looking at anecdotal cases to support a demand
letter on long gun multiple sales. Thanks Mark R. Chait Assistant
Director Field Operations
```

This July 14, 2010, email from ATF Field Operations Assistant Director Mark Chait to ATF Phoenix Special Agent in Charge Bill Newell shows Chait asking Newell for evidence that long gun sales came from the same federally licensed firearms dealer, in order to make the case for a new long gun reporting measure.

APPENDIX 15

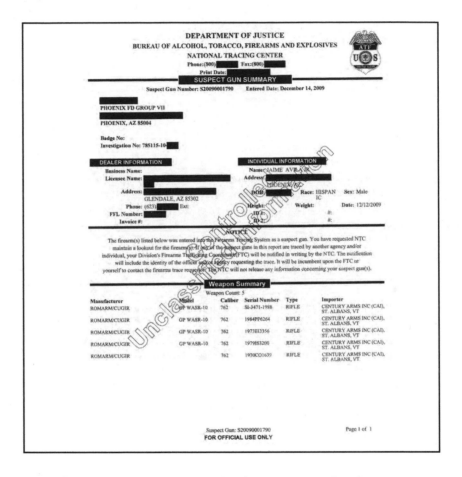

DEPARTMENT OF JUSTICE
BUREAU OF ALCOHOL, TOBACCO, FIREARMS AND EXPLOSIVES
NATIONAL TRACING CENTER

Phone:(800)   Fax:(800)
Print Date:

SUSPECT GUN SUMMARY

Suspect Gun Number: S20090001790   Entered Date: December 14, 2009

PHOENIX FD GROUP VII

PHOENIX, AZ 85004

Badge No:
Investigation No: 785115-10-

DEALER INFORMATION   **INDIVIDUAL INFORMATION**

Business Name: Name: JAIME AVILA JR
Licensee Name: Address:
                                                            PHOENIX, AZ
Address: DOB: Race: HISPAN   Sex: Male
        GLENDALE, AZ 85302   IC
Phone: (623)   Ext: Height: Weight: Date: 12/12/2009
FFL Number: ID 1:   ft:
Invoice #:   ID 2:   #:

NOTICE

The firearm(s) listed below was entered into the Firearms Tracing System as a suspect gun. You have requested NTC maintain a lookout for the firearm(s). If any of the suspect guns in this report are traced by another agency and/or individual, your Division's Firearms Trafficking Coordinator(FTC) will be notified in writing by the NTC. The notification will include the identity of the officer and/or agency requesting the trace. It will be incumbent upon the FTC or yourself to contact the firearms trace requestor. The NTC will not release any information concerning your suspect gun(s).

Weapon Summary
Weapon Count: 5

Manufacturer	Model	Caliber	Serial Number	Type	Importer
ROMARM/CUGIR	GP WASR-10	762	SI-3471-1988	RIFLE	CENTURY ARMS INC (CAI), ST. ALBANS, VT
ROMARM/CUGIR	GP WASR-10	762	1984PF6264	RIFLE	CENTURY ARMS INC (CAI), ST. ALBANS, VT
ROMARM/CUGIR	GP WASR-10	762	1973EI3356	RIFLE	CENTURY ARMS INC (CAI), ST. ALBANS, VT
ROMARM/CUGIR	GP WASR-10	762	1979IS3200	RIFLE	CENTURY ARMS INC (CAI), ST. ALBANS, VT
ROMARM/CUGIR		762	1970CO1639	RIFLE	CENTURY ARMS INC (CAI), ST. ALBANS, VT

Suspect Gun: S20090001790   Page 1 of 1
FOR OFFICIAL USE ONLY

One of many suspect gun summaries the ATF accumulated on straw purchaser Jaime Avila. The National Tracing Center traced the guns listed here to a gun dealer in Glendale, Arizona. The dealer was most likely Lone Wolf Trading Company, although the name of the business and the license name have been redacted.

APPENDIX 16

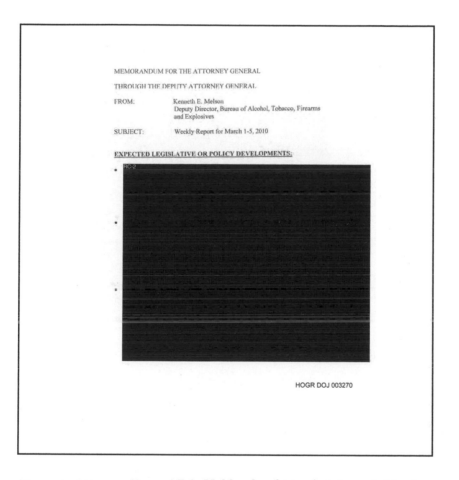

Memo to Attorney General Eric Holder dated March 1 through March 5, 2010, from then ATF Acting Director Kenneth Melson. The memo bullet points redacted material under "expected legislative or policy developments" as a result of ATF activities.

APPENDIX 17

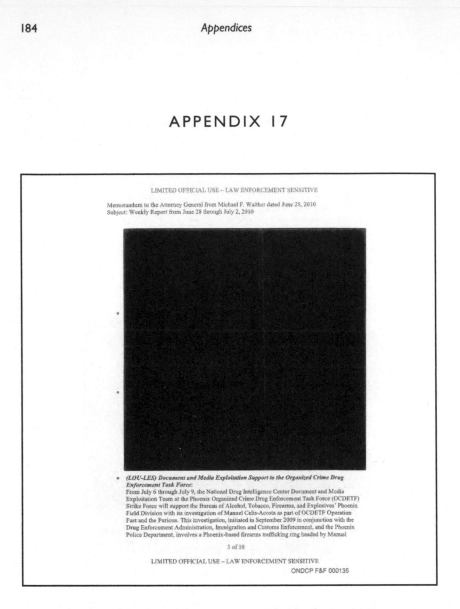

Yet another heavily redacted document provided by the Justice Department to the House Oversight Committee. This is a memo to Attorney General Eric Holder, dated June 28, 2010–July 2, 2010. The memo discusses Operation Fast and Furious as an OCDETF operation, meaning the program spanned multiple government agencies, including ATF and DOJ. The memo notes Fast and Furious started in September 2009. Although the memo is addressed directly to Holder, he denies knowing about Operation Fast and Furious until after Brian Terry's murder.

APPENDIX 18

A heavily redacted memo to Attorney General Eric Holder, dated August 2 through August 6, 2010.

APPENDIX 19

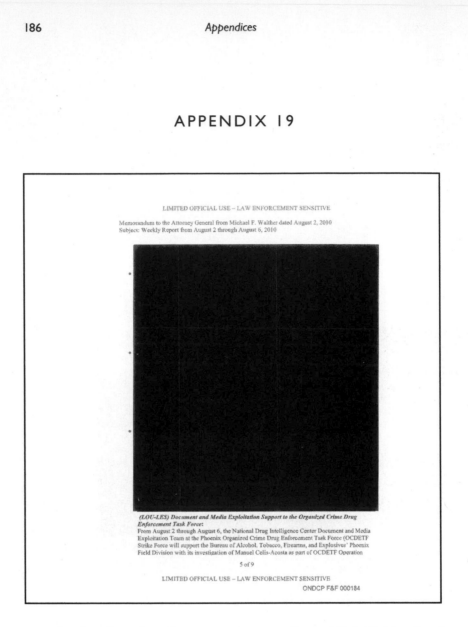

LIMITED OFFICIAL USE – LAW ENFORCEMENT SENSITIVE

Memorandum to the Attorney General from Michael F. Walther dated August 2, 2010
Subject: Weekly Report from August 2 through August 6, 2010

(LOU-LES) Document and Media Exploitation Support to the Organized Crime Drug Enforcement Task Force:
From August 2 through August 6, the National Drug Intelligence Center Document and Media Exploitation Team at the Phoenix Organized Crime Drug Enforcement Task Force (OCDETF Strike Force will support the Bureau of Alcohol. Tobacco, Firearms, and Explosives' Phoenix Field Division with its investigation of Manuel Celis-Acosta as part of OCDETF Operation

5 of 9

LIMITED OFFICIAL USE – LAW ENFORCEMENT SENSITIVE
ONDCP F&F 000184

Another heavily redacted memo to Attorney General Eric Holder, dated August 2 through August 6, 2010. Both memos are presumed to mention Fast and Furious.

APPENDIX 20

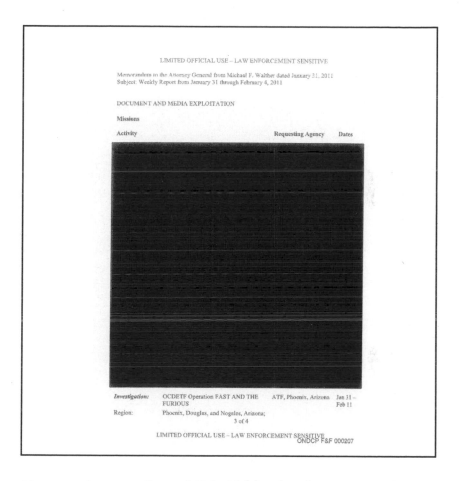

Memorandum to the Attorney General from Michael F. Walther dated January 31, 2011
Subject: Weekly Report from January 31 through February 4, 2011

DOCUMENT AND MEDIA EXPLOITATION

Missions

Activity   Requesting Agency   Dates

| *Investigation:* | OCDETF Operation FAST AND THE FURIOUS | ATF, Phoenix, Arizona | Jan 31 – Feb 11 |
| Region: | Phoenix, Douglas, and Nogales, Arizona; | | |

3 of 4

Memo to Attorney General Eric Holder dated January 31 through February 4, 2011. The memo notes, "Investigation: OCDETF Operation FAST AND THE FURIOUS." Although the memo is addressed directly to Holder, he denies knowing about Operation Fast and Furious until a few months before congressional testimony on May 3, 2011.

APPENDIX 21

LIMITED OFFICIAL USE – LAW ENFORCEMENT SENSITIVE

Memorandum to the Attorney General from Michael F. Walther dated January 31, 2011
Subject: Weekly Report from January 31 through February 4, 2011

Activity		Requesting Agency	Dates
	and El Paso, Texas		
Targets:	Manuel CELIA-ACOSTA		
Drugs/Crime:	Straw purchase of firearms for SINALOA CARTEL		
Participants:	ATF		

4 of 4

LIMITED OFFICIAL USE – LAW ENFORCEMENT SENSITIVE
ONDCP F&F 000208

A heavily redacted memo to Attorney General Eric Holder, dated January 31 through February 4, 2011.

APPENDIX 22

6. Continued Pursuit of Corrupt Public Officials Who Facilitate the Drug Trade

7. Merida

This heavily redacted document mentions the Merida Initiative, a funding agreement between the United States and Mexico to combat drug, human, and weapons trafficking, which may have been threatened if the Mexican government continued to react strongly to Fast and Furious.

ACKNOWLEDGMENTS

Anybody who has written a book knows it cannot be done alone. Keith Urbahn and Matt Latimer of Javelin came to me with the idea of taking my reporting on Operation Fast and Furious and turning it into a book. They helped me shape the narrative and have been a source of counsel, perspective, and encouragement throughout the process. Thank you for believing in me.

My thanks go to Michelle Malkin for introducing me to the world of authors. She brought my name to the attention of publishers. For years I have looked up to Michelle, like so many do, as a giant of a role model. She gave me advice, suggestions, and support about how to get this project done.

To Regnery, thank you for taking a chance on a young journalist and blogger. I appreciate the opportunity to be on your list of published works. Harry Crocker and Mary Beth Baker were superb editors.

My boss, Jonathan Garthwaite at Townhall, is a saint. Not only did he hire me fresh out of college, but since then has had nothing but full faith in my ability to succeed. He has given me the creative freedom to do so. Because Jonathan has had the courtesy to take me under his wing and to allow me to write under the Townhall masthead, I've been able to experience so many things I never thought were possible.

To Chris Field, who published my first big story about Fast and Furious in *Townhall Magazine* and who has served as a close friend and mentor, thank you for always giving me a hard time.

Much gratitude goes to the rest of my amazing and supportive Townhall family. Mary Crookston deserves special recognition for her contribution to this book by transcribing a number of interviews and hearings, in addition to digging through endless amounts of White House visitor logs for me. Thank you for your patience and support throughout this process. I could not be blessed with better friends and people to work with.

For those in the media who continue to push this story forward, thank you and keep up the good work. To Sharyl Attkisson of CBS News, without you this story would never have received the attention it has so far. Had you not had the patience to pore over documents and the courage take on government officials, the Terry family would never have known what the true circumstances surrounding their son's murder were. Many thanks to Michelle Malkin, the *Daily Caller*'s Matthew Boyle, Big Journalism's Mary Chastain, Pajama Media's Bob Owens, *Los Angeles Times* reporter Richard Serrano, NRA News Radio host Cam Edwards, bloggers David Codrea and Mike Vanderboegh, and the blogosphere in general for not letting the story die.

I also owe a huge debt to Jon Justice (Jon Logiudice), host of the *Jon Justice Show* in Tucson, who first taught me how to expose corruption during my time as a college student. I've had various teachers and mentors who also deserve recognition: Tom Tripp, Professor Kevin Kemper, Rogelio Garcia, Hank Kenski.

I don't often thank politicians for their work, but House Oversight Chairman Darrell Issa, Senator Charles Grassley, and their staffs deserve an enormous thanks from the American people for vowing to get the bottom of this horrendous scandal. They are true watchdogs of government and deserve the utmost respect. Thanks to Representative Jason Chaffetz and Representative Trey Gowdy for always asking the best questions.

To Jay Dobyns and Vince Cefalu, this one's for you. We know this whole thing is just getting started. To John Dodson, Peter Forcelli, and all the whistleblowers, thank you for having the courage to speak the truth in the face of retaliation. Thank you for doing the right thing, even when the right thing wasn't the easy thing to do. You are true examples of courage through strength.

To the victims of Fast and Furious, who made writing this book worthwhile, no words of gratitude can ease the pain you have endured, no book can make things right. For Brian Terry, honesty was important. It was everything. His parents, Josephine and Kent, and the rest of his family, deserve to know what happened to their son. His death and honor deserve no less than the truth. The same goes for the family of Jaime Zapata and the countless, faceless lives lost in Mexico.

Life today wouldn't be what it is without my parents, Paul and Peggy. Thank you for always pushing me toward challenges, not away from them. Without your encouragement and support throughout the years, dreams I never realized I had, my career wouldn't be possible. Thank you for instilling in me a strong work ethic, a hard streak of perseverance, and the will to fight important battles. For my brother, Paul, thanks for being my best friend and teaching me that life doesn't always have to be serious. Thanks to my Great Aunt Mary Roby for being a shining example of what a strong woman should look like, and to my Great Uncle Fred for being a pillar of strength for all of us. To my Great Uncle Clarence Duncan, thank you for teaching me the lesson of humility. My friends who feel like family deserve an award for patience during my absence over the past few months.

To any I have forgotten, please know you are greatly appreciated.

NOTES

Chapter One

1. Dylan Smith, "Star: Krentz murder suspect being sought in U.S.," *Tucson Sentinel*, May 3, 2010; available online at: http://www.tucsonsentinel.com/local/report/050310_krentz/star-krentz-murder-suspect-being-sought-us/.
2. SecuretheBorderAz, "Brewer to Obama, Warning Signs Are Not Enough," video retrieved February 6, 2011; available online at: http://www.youtube.com/watch?v=bzDlN7VLmXQ.
3. Leo Banks, "Smugglers' Paradise," *Tucson Weekly*, November 25, 2010; available online at: http://www.tucsonweekly.com/tucson/smugglers-paradise/Content?oid=2365902.
4. Daily Mail Reporter, "Fat, Skin and Bones Found in Some of Mexican Drug Cartel's Body Handler, 'The Stew-Maker,'" *Daily Mail*, February 22, 2011; available online at: http://www.dailymail.co.uk/news/article-1359430/Fat-skin-bones-home-Mexican-drug-cartels-Stew-maker.html.

Chapter Two

1. Katharine Seelye and Jeff Zeleny, "On the Defensive, Obama Calls His Words Ill-Chosen," *New York Times*, April 13, 2008; available online at: http://www.nytimes.com/2008/04/13/us/politics/13campaign.html?pagewanted=all.

2.   Barack Obama, *Dreams from My Father* (Crown, reprint edition, 2007), p. 277.

3.   Ibid., p. 399.

4.   Caroline McKay and Benjamin Scuderi, "From Harvard to D.C. and Back Again," *Harvard Crimson*, April 7, 2007; available online at: http://www.thecrimson.com/article/2011/4/7/tribe-summers-washington-professor/.

5.   Independent Voters of Illinois Independent Precinct Organization, http://www.iviipo.org/Civil.htm.

6.   D'Angelo Gore, "500 Percent Ammo Tax?" FactCheck.org, June 22, 2009; available online at: http://www.factcheck.org/2009/06/500-percent-ammo-tax/.

7.   Chris W. Cox, "Obama and Guns," *Front Page Magazine*, November 2, 2008; available online at: http://archive.frontpagemag.com/readArticle.aspx?ARTID=32954.

8.   Jerome Corsi , *The Obama Nation* (Pocket Star, 2010), 241–242.

9.   "Third Illinois 2004 Senate Debate: Barack Obama vs. Alan Keyes, Oct. 21, 2004," *On the Issues*; available online at: http://www.issues2000.org/IL_2004_Senate_3rd.htm.

10.   U.S. Senate Roll Call Votes 109th Congress–1st Session, Senate Roll Call Lists/ Call Vote; available online at: http://www.senate.gov/legislative/LIS/roll_call_lists/roll_call_vote_cfm.cfm?congress=109&session=1&vote=00219.

11.   "2008 Democratic debate in Las Vegas, Jan. 15, 2008, last debate prior to Nevada primary," *On the Issues*; available online at: http://www.issues2000.org/2008_Dems_Las_Vegas.htm.

12.   "Fact Check: Does Obama want to ban guns and rifles?" CNN Politics, September 23, 2008; available online at: http://politicalticker.blogs.cnn.com/2008/09/23/fact-check-does-obama-want-to-ban-guns-and-rifles/.

13.   Teddy Davis and Talal Al-Khatib, "Obama Forgets Writing on Gun Questionnaire," ABC News, April 17, 2008; available online at: http://abcnews.go.com/blogs/politics/2008/04/obama-forgets-w/.

14.   Viveco Novak, "Gunning for Obama," FactCheck.org, May 6, 2008; available online at: http://www.factcheck.org/2008/05/gunning-for-obama/.

15.   Ben Smith, "Chicago activists doubt Obama's explanation on questionnaire," *POLITICO*, December 7, 2007; available online at: http://www.politico.com/blogs/bensmith/1207/Chicago_activists_doubt_Obamas_answers_on_questionnaire.html.

16.   "2008 Democratic debate in Las Vegas, Jan. 15, 2008, last debate prior to the Nevada primary," op. cit., 14.

17.   Compiled from wire reports and other media sources, "Obama Nominates Eric Holder as Nation's Top Law Enforcement Official," PBS *News Hour*, December

1, 2008; available online at: http://www.pbs.org/newshour/indepth_coverage/white_house/transition2008/holder_profile.html.

18. Javier C. Hernandez, "Holder, High Achiever Poised to Scale New Heights," *New York Times*, November 30, 2008; available online at: http://www.nytimes.com/2008/12/01/nyregion/01holder.html?pagewanted=all.

19. Ronald Kolb, "The Ethics of Eric Holder," *American Thinker*, December 4, 2011; available online at: http://www.americanthinker.com/2011/12/the_ethics_of_eric_holder.html.

20. "White House to Plan 'All-Out Offensive on Guns,'" *Washington Post*, December 15, 1999; available online at: http://articles.latimes.com/1999/dec/15/news/mn-44082.

21. "Shocker: Obama's Attorney General Pick Is A Gun-Grabber," *SayAnythingBlog*, November 19, 2008, http://sayanythingblog.com/entry/shocker_obamas_attorney_general_pick_is_a_gun_grabber/.

22. "Eric Holder's Politics," *Wall Street Journal*, December 4, 2008.

23. "Shocker: Obama's Attorney General Pick is a Gun-Grabber," op. cit., 25.

24. "Governors increase aid, fight violence," *Rocky Point Vacation Guide*; available online at: http://www.visitrockypoint.com/governors-increase-aid-fight-violence.

25. "Holder admits 'mistakes' in Rich pardon," CNN Politics, January 15, 2009; available online at: http://articles.cnn.com/2009-01-15/politics/holder.hearings_1_marc-rich-pardon-rich-case?_s=PM:POLITICS.

26. Letter from GOP lawyers to Senator Patrick Leahy and Arlen Specter, January 2009. Eric Holder recommendation.

27. Department of Homeland Security, Rightwing Extremism: Current Economic and Political Climate Fueling Resurgence in Radicalization and Recruitment (2009), pp. 2, 4, 7; available online at: www.fas.org/irp/eprint/rightwing.pdf.

28. "Statement by U.S. Department of Homeland Security Secretary Janet Napolitano on the Threat of Right-Wing Extremism," Department of Homeland Security, press release, April 15, 2009; available online at: http://www.dhs.gov/ynews/releases/pr_1239817562001.shtm.

29. "Napolitano apologizes to American Legion," Associated Press, April 24, 2009; available online at: http://www.azcentral.com/news/articles/2009/04/24/20090424Napolitano24-ON.html.

30. Jason Ryan, "Obama to Seek New Assault Weapons Ban," ABC News, February 25, 2009; available online at: http://abcnews.go.com/Politics/story?id=6960824&page=1.

Chapter Three

1.   Post Politics, People in the News, "David Ogden," *Washington Post*, February 2010; available online at: http://www.washingtonpost.com/politics/david-ogden/gIQAwads9O_topic.html.

2.   Tom McClusky, "Change Watch Backgrounder: David Ogden," Family Research Center, February 2, 2009; available online at: http://www.frcblog.com/2009/02/change-watch-backgrounder-david-ogden/.

3.   Post Politics, People in the News, "David Ogden," op. cit., 1.

4.   Deputy Attorney General David Ogden Press Conference March 24, 2010.

5.   Ibid.

6.   Ashley Fantz, "The Mexico Drug War: Bodies for Billions," CNN *World*, January 20, 2012; available online at: http://www.cnn.com/2012/01/15/world/mexico-drug-war-essay/index.html.

7.   "Testimony of Secretary Napolitano before the Senate Committee on the Judiciary, 'Oversight of the Department of Homeland Security,'" Homeland Security, May 6, 2009; available online at: http://www.dhs.gov/ynews/testimony/testimony_1241706742872.shtm.

8.   Andrea Mitchell, "Secretary of State Hillary Clinton," MSNBC, March 26, 2009.

9.   Ibid.

10.   Eric Holder, "Attorney General Eric Holder at the Mexico/United States Arms Trafficking Conference," Cuernavaca, Mexico, April 2, 2009; available online at: http://www.justice.gov/ag/speeches/2009/ag-speech-090402.html.

11.   Department of Justice, *Fighting Criminal Activity on the U.S. Southwest Border Fact Sheet* (2009), www.justice.gov/jmd/2009factsheets/pdf/rollout-fact-sheet-swb.pdf, p. 2.

12.   "Joint Press Conference with President Barack Obama and President Felipe Calderón of Mexico," Los Pinos, Mexico City, Mexico, April 16, 2009; available online at: http://www.whitehouse.gov/the-press-office/joint-press-conference-with-president-barack-obama-and-president-felipe-calderon-me.

13.   "ATF Mexico Gun Statistics Flawed," Office of Senator Chuck Grassley press release, November 15, 2011; available online at: http://www.grassley.senate.gov/news/Article.cfm?customel_dataPageID_1502=37872.

14.   Embassy Mexico 232113, October 2009, "Mexico Arms Trafficking: Access to Confiscated," WikiLeaks; available online at: http://www.wikileaks.org/cable/2009/10/09MEXICO3114.html#.

15.   Ibid.

16. Sharyl Attkisson, "Legal U.S. gun sales to Mexico arming cartels," CBS News, December 6, 2011; available online at: http://www.cbsnews.com/ 8301-500202_162-57337289/legal-u.s-gun-sales-to-mexico-arming-cartels/.

17. Ibid.

18. EFE, "Mexican cartels get heavy weapons from CentAm cables say," Fox News Latino, March 30, 2011; available online at: http://latino.foxnews.com/latino/ news/2011/03/30/mexican-cartels-heavy-weapons-centam-cables-say/.

19. Embassy Mexico 232113, October 2009, "Mexico Arms Trafficking: Access to Confiscated," op. cit., 14.

20. Erik Larson, "ATF Under Siege," *Time*, July 24, 1995; available online at: http:// www.time.com/time/magazine/article/0,9171,983197,00.html.

21. Internal prison documents, letters, and U.S. Department of Justice Office of the Inspector General, OIG Report on Allegations by Bureau of Alcohol, Tobacco, Firearms, and Explosives Special Agent Jay Dobyns, OSC File No. DI-07-0367, September 22, 2008; available online at: www.osc.gov/ . . . /09-19%20DI-07- 0367%20Agency%20Report.pdf.

22. U.S. Department of Justice Office of the Inspector General, *OIG Report on Allegations by Bureau of Alcohol, Tobacco, Firearms, and Explosives Special Agent Jay Dobyns.*

23. Ibid.

24. Phone Interview with Jay Dobyns by Katie Pavlich, October 28, 2011.

25. Ibid.

26. Interview with Peter Forcelli by Katie Pavlich, November 28, 2011.

27. Interviews with Jay Dobyns, John Dodson, Vince Cefalu, and Peter Forcelli. All confirmed this point.

28. Quin Hillyer, "Deep Corruption at the Obama Justice Department," *American Spectator*, September 15, 2011; available online at: http://spectator.org/ archives/2011/09/15/deep-corruption-at-the-obama-j.

29. Mayors Against Illegal Guns, "Mayors Against Illegal Guns Releases New Report on Crime Guns Trafficked into Mexico Fueling Drug Cartel Violence," press release, September 7, 2010; available online at: http://www. mayorsagainstillegalguns.org/html/media-center/pr007-10.shtml.

30. "Ranking Member Grassley Presentation Material at House Oversight Hearing on Operation Fast and Furious," prepared statement of Senator Chuck Grassley before the United States House of Representatives Committee on Oversight and Government Reform, June 15, 2011; available online at: http://www.grassley. senate.gov/news/Article.cfm?customel_dataPageID_1502=35387.

31. Interview of anonymous source by Katie Pavlich, December 11, 2011.

32.   Ibid.

33.   United States Congress Joint Staff Report, *The Department of Justice's Operation Fast and Furious: Accounts of ATF Agents*, June 14, 2011; available online at: http://oversight.house.gov/images/stories/Reports/ATF_Report.pdf, p. 15.

34.   ATF Briefing paper, "Phoenix Field Division Phoenix Group VII (Gunrunner/Strike Force)," January 8, 2010; available online at: www.cbsnews.com/htdocs/pdf/110504_briefing_papers.pdf.

35.   Interview with Peter Forcelli by Katie Pavlich, November 28, 2011.

36.   Ibid.

37.   Ibid.

38.   Dennis Wagner, "Burke of Fast and Furious had anti-gun history," *Arizona Republic*, January 28, 2012.

39.   Interview with Peter Forcelli by Katie Pavlich, November 28, 2011.

40.   Ibid.

41.   Ibid.

42.   Rick Young, "Phoenix, AZ: The Story of X Caliber Guns," PBS News *Frontline*, February 3, 2011; available online at: http://www.pbs.org/wgbh/pages/frontline/gunrunners-mexico/phoenix/. And interview with Peter Forcelli by Katie Pavlich, November 28, 2011.

43.   Ibid.

44.   "Operation Fast and Furious: Reckless Decisions, Tragic Outcomes," before the House Committee on Government Oversight and Reform, 112th Cong., June 15, 2011, opening statement of ATF Special Agent Peter Forcelli.

45.   Ibid.

46.   ATF Briefing paper, "Phoenix Field Division Phoenix Group VII (Gunrunner/Strike Force)," op. cit., 34.

47.   Richard A. Serrano, "Gun store owner had misgivings about ATF sting," *Los Angeles Times*, September 11, 2011; available online at: http://articles.latimes.com/2011/sep/11/nation/la-na-atf-guns-20110912.

48.   Ibid.

49.   United States Congress Joint Staff Report, *The Department of Justice's Operation Fast and Furious: Accounts of ATF Agents*, p. 16.

50.   "New documents reveal Federal Firearms Licensee voiced concerns with Fast and Furious strategy," Office of Senator Charles Grassley, April 14, 2011; available online at: http://www.grassley.senate.gov/news/Article.cfm?customel_dataPageID_1502=33847#_ftnref3.

51.   Interview with anonymous source by Katie Pavlich, December 11, 2011.

52.   "Operation Fast and Furious: Reckless Decisions, Tragic Outcomes," op. cit., 47.

Chapter Four

1. ATF agents are stationed in international locations to assist foreign governments with prevention of illegal firearms trafficking, explosives training, combat of violent gangs, and criminal investigation training among other things.
2. ATF International Offices, http://www.atf.gov/field/international/.
3. United States Congress, *The Department of Justice's Operation Fast and Furious: Fueling Cartel Violence*, July 26, 2011; available online at: http://oversight.house.gov/images/stories/Reports/FINAL_FINAL.pdf, p. 28.
4. Ibid., p. 29.
5. "Operation Fast and Furious: The Other Side of the Border," Oversight and Government Reform Committee, July 26, 2011, 112th Cong., statement of Darren Gil, former ATF Attaché to Mexico.
6. Ibid.
7. United States Congress, *The Department of Justice's Operation Fast and Furious: Fueling Cartel Violence* op. cit., 3.
8. Gary Kleck, "The Myth of Big-Time Gun Trafficking," *Wall Street Journal*, May 21, 2011; available online at: http://online.wsj.com/article/SB10001424052748704904604576333443343499926.html.
9. Katie Pavlich, "ATF Director Watching Cartels Buy Guns from Washington DC," *Townhall*, June 15, 2011; available online at: http://townhall.com/tipsheet/katiepavlich/2011/06/15/atf_director_watching_cartels_buy_guns_from_washington_dc.
10. "Operation Fast and Furious: Reckless Decisions, Tragic Outcomes," 112th Cong., June 15, 2011, statement of Charles Grassley, Senator.
11. United States Congress, *The Department of Justice's Operation Fast and Furious: Fueling Cartel Violence*, op. cit., 3.
12. *U.S. Attorney's Criminal Resource Manuel*, Title 9 Chapter 9-7.000, "Electronic Surveillance."
13. Interview with Peter Forcelli by Katie Pavlich, November 28, 2011.
14. Ibid.
15. Ibid.
16. David J. Voth email to Phoenix Grup VII, March 12, 2010; available online at: http://www.cbsnews.com/htdocs/pdf/Grassley_2011_03_page14.pdf.
17. United States Congress, *The Department of Justice's Operation Fast and Furious: Fueling Cartel Violence*, op. cit., 3.
18. Ibid.
19. Ibid.

20. United States Congress, *The Department of Justice's Operation Fast and Furious-Fueling Cartel Violence*, op. cit., 3.

21. "Mexico drugs war murders data mapped," *The Guardian*, January 14, 2011; available online at: http://www.guardian.co.uk/news/datablog/2011/jan/14/mexico-drug-war-murders-map.

22. Email from David Voth, April 2, 2010, to Group VII.

23. Dennis Wagner, "ATF gun probe: Behind the Fall of Operation Fast and Furious," *Arizona Republican*, November 27, 2011.

24. United States Congress, Joint Staff Report: *The Department of Justice's Operation Fast and Furious: Accounts of ATF Agents*, June 14, 2011; available online at: http://www.scribd.com/doc/79704769/The-Department-of-Justice%E2%80%99s-Operation-Fast-and-Furious-Accounts-of-ATF-Agents-GunWalker-Operations.

25. "Operation Fast and Furious: Reckless Decisions, Tragic Outcomes," 112th Cong., June 15, 2011, statement of ATF Special Agent Olindo Casa.

26. Email to David Voth from cooperating FfL, June 17, 2010.

27. Email to cooperating FfL from David Voth, June 17, 2010.

28. Email to cooperating FfL from David Voth, August 25, 2010.

29. Interview with anonymous source by Katie Pavlich, December 11, 2011.

30. Michael Isikoff, "Obama Gets Gun-Shy," *Newsweek*, April 10, 2009; available online at: http://www.thedailybeast.com/newsweek/2009/04/10/obama-gets-gun-shy.html.

31. Jason Horowitz, "Over a barrel? Meet White House gun policy advisor Steve Croley," *Washington Post*, April 11, 2011; available online at: http://www.washingtonpost.com/lifestyle/style/over-a-barrel-meet-white-house-gun-policy-adviser-steve-croley/2011/04/04/AFt9EKND_story.html.

32. Email from Mark Chait to Bill Newell, cc: William McMahon, July 14, 2010.

33. See image of Gary Grindler's handwritten notes in photo section.

34. "Mayors Against Illegal Guns Releases New Report on Crime Guns Trafficked into Mexico Fueling Drug Cartel Violence," Mayors Against Illegal Guns, September 7, 2010; available online at: http://www.mayorsagainstillegalguns.org/html/media-center/pr007-10.shtml.

35. United States Congress, Joint Staff Report *The Department of Justice's Operation Fast and Furious: Accounts of ATF Agents* op.cit., p. 24.

36. Katie Pavlich, "Fast and Furious, Using Humans as Collateral Damage," *Townhall*, September 27, 2011; available online at: http://townhall.com/columnists/katiepavlich/2011/09/27/fast_and_furious_using_humans_as_collateral_damage/page/full/.

37. Sharyl Attkisson, "Agent: I was ordered to let guns into Mexico," CBS News, March 3, 2011; available online at: http://www.cbsnews.com/stories/2011/03/03/eveningnews/main20039031.shtml?tag=contentMain;contentBody.

Chapter Five

1. Email exchange available online at: http://www.grassley.senate.gov/judiciary/upload/Holder-11-28-11-Facts-are-Stubborn-Things-Deputy-Chief-of-Staff-knowledge.pdf.
2. "Border Patrol Agent Killed—Full Coverage," KVOA News 4, December 15, 2010; available online at: http://www.kvoa.com/pages/border-patrol-agent-shot-full-coverage/.
3. Jonathan Clark, Manuel C. Coppola, and Terry Ketron, "Authorities hunt for suspect in Border Patrol agent's killing," *Nogales International*, December 15, 2010; available online at: http://www.nogalesinternational.com/news/breaking_news/authorities-hunt-for-suspect-in-border-patrol-agent-s-killing/article_1156bc3c-8995-529e-ae46-4c3d8cf396d0.html.
4. Email to Dennis Burke from Monty Wilkinson, December 15, 2010.
5. Email to Ann Scheel from Dennis Burke, December 15, 2010.
6. Email to Arizona U.S. Attorney Dennis Burke from Matthew Chandler, December 15, 2010.
7. Press Conference on Murder of BP Agent Brian Terry in Arizona, December 17, 2010.
8. Email to Dennis Burke and Ann Scheel from Shelley Clemens, December 15, 2010.
9. Email to ATF ASAC Charles Smith from El Paso ATF SAC Glen Cook, December 17, 2010.
10. Email to Bill McMahon from Bill Newell, December 21, 2010.
11. Email to Gary Grindler from Brad Smith, December 17, 2010.
12. "Operation Fast and Furious: Reckless Decisions, Tragic Outcomes," 112th Cong., June 15, 2011, statement of Josephine Terry (Brian Terry's mother).
13. Department of Homeland Security, "Statement by Homeland Security Secretary Janet Napolitano on the Death of Border Patrol Agent Brian A. Terry," press release, December 15, 2010; available online at: http://www.dhs.gov/ynews/releases/pr_1292436162687.shtm.
14. Joel Waldman, "Interview with Janet Napolitano," KGUN 9 News, December 23, 2010.

15. Ibid.

16. "Who is Jared Loughner? Friends Reveal Alienation," CBS News/Associated Press, January 10, 2011; available online at: http://www.cbsnews.com/8301-201_162-7229463.html.

17. "Jared Loughner's Friend Tells GMA: 'He Did Not Watch TV, He Disliked the News,'" Mediate.com., January 12, 2011; available online at: http://www.mediaite.com/tv/jared-laughners-friend-tells-gma-he-did-not-watch-tv-he-disliked-the-news/.

18. "Who is Jared Loughner? Friends Reveal Alienation," CBS News/Associated Press, January 10, 2011.

19. United States Congress Joint Staff Report, *The Department of Justice's Operation Fast and Furious: Accounts of ATF Agents*, June 14, 2011; available online at: http://oversight.house.gov/images/stories/Reports/ATF_Report.pdf.

20. David Codrea, "A journalist's guide to 'Project Gunwalker'—Part One," *Gun Rights Examiner*, February 1, 2011; available online at: http://www.examiner.com/gun-rights-in-national/a-journalist-s-guide-to-project-gunwalker.

21. Ibid.

22. "Grand Juries Indict 34 Suspects in Drug and Firearms Trafficking Organization," Bureau of Alcohol, Tobacco, Firearms and Explosives and the Arizona U.S. Attorney's Office, press conference, January 25, 2011.

23. Bill Newell, quoted in Dennis Wagner, "ATF gun probe: Behind the fall of Operation Fast and Furious," *Arizona Republic*, February 23, 2012; available online at: http://www.azcentral.com/arizonarepublic/news/articles/2011/11/12/20111112atf-gun-probe-operation-fast-and-furious-fall.html.

24. Ibid.

Chapter Six

1. Mike Vanderboegh, "Pure Fact Verified: The ATF Scandal That's Going to Guarantee Oversight Hearings," *Sipsey Street Irregulars*, January 5, 2011; available online at: http://sipseystreetirregulars.blogspot.com/2011/01/pure-fact-verified-atf-scandal-thats.html.

2. Interview with anonymous source by Katie Pavlich, December 11, 2011.

3. Letter from Senator Charles Grassley to ATF Acting Director Kenneth Melson, January 27, 2011; available online at: http://grassley.senate.gov/about/upload/Judiciary-01-27-11-letter-to-ATF-SW-Border-strategy.pdf.

4. Letter from Congressman Charles Grassley to Kenneth E. Melson, Acting Director Bureau of Alcohol, Tobacco, Firearms, and Explosives, January 31, 2011; available online at: http://www.grassley.senate.gov/about/loader.cfm?csModule=security/getfile&pageid=31353.

5.   Senator Chuck Grassley, "Facts are STUBBORN Things…The Justice Department Tries to Have it Both Ways," press release, December 2, 2011; available online at: http://www.grassley.senate.gov/news/Article.cfm?customeI_dataPageID_1502=38110.

6.   Email from Arizona U.S. Attorney Dennis Burke to Jason Weinstein, January 31, 2011.

7.   Email from Deputy Attorney General Lanny Breuer to ATF Acting Director Kenneth Melson, February 1, 2011.

8.   Senator Chuck Grassley, "Facts are STUBBORN Things…The Justice Department Tries to Have it Both Ways," op. cit., 5.

9.   Katherine Corcoran, "Jaime Zapata, U.S. Immigration And Customs Enforcement Agent, Killed In Mexico," Associated Press, February 16, 2011; available online at: www.huffingtonpost.com/2011/02/16/jamie-zapata-killed-mexico-us-immigration_n_824084.html.

10.   "U.S. Rep Says ICE Agents Were Ambushed by Zetas in Mexico," Associated Press, February 17, 2011; available online at: http://www.foxnews.com/world/2011/02/17/rep-says-ice-agents-ambushed-zetas-mexico/.

11.   "Secretary Napolitano and Attorney General Holder form Joint Task Force to Assist Mexico's Investigation into Yesterday's Shooting of Two ICE Agents in Mexico," Department of Homeland Security, press release, February 16, 2011; available online at: http://www.dhs.gov/ynews/releases/pr_1297887776389.shtm.

12.   Ibid.

13.   Cam Edwards, "Carter's Country Gun Store Attorney Dick DeGuerin," NRA News radio, *Cam & Company*, July 27, 2011; listen online at: http://www.nranews.com/videos/4939.aspx.

14.   Interview with anonymous source by Katie Pavlich.

15.   Richard A. Serrano, "Family of U.S. agent slain in Mexico demands to know gun source," *Los Angeles Times*, July 17, 2011; available online at: http://articles.latimes.com/2011/jul/17/nation/la-na-guns-cartel-20110718.

16.   Sharyl Attkisson, "Gunwalker: The smoking gun and Jaime Zapata," CBS News, November 7, 2011; available online at: http://www.cbsnews.com/video/watch/?id=7387457n.

17.   Sharyl Attkisson, "Agent: I was ordered to let U.S. guns into Mexico," CBS News, March 3, 2011; available online at: http://www.cbsnews.com/stories/2011/03/03/eveningnews/main20039031.shtml.

18.   *The Laura Ingraham Show*, October 4, 2011.

19.   Ibid.

20. Charlie Savage, "Under Partisan Fire Eric Holder Soldiers On," *New York Times*, December 18, 2011; available online at: http://www.nytimes.com/2011/12/18/us/politics/under-partisan-fire-eric-holder-soldiers-on.html?pagewanted=all.

21. Editorial, "How Congress can empower the ATF," *Washington Post*, June 26, 2011; available online at: http://www.washingtonpost.com/opinions/2011/06/21/AGaGOcmH_story.html.

22. Peter Maer, "Obama meets with Calderon at critical juncture in U.S.-Mexican relations," CBS News, March 3, 2011; available online at: http://www.cbsnews.com/8301-503544_162-20038452-503544.html.

23. James V. Grimaldi and Sari Horwitz, "As Mexico drug violence runs rampant, U.S. guns tied to crime south of border," *Washington Post*, December 15, 2010; available online at: http://www.washingtonpost.com/wp-dyn/content/article/2010/12/12/AR2010121202663.html?hpid=topnews&sid=ST2010121203267.

24. Ibid.

25. Stephanie Mencimer, "Conservatives Are Gunning for Eric Holder," *Mother Jones*, December 7, 2011; available online at: http://motherjones.com/politics/2011/12/why-republicans-are-gunning-eric-holder-operation-fast-furious.

26. Ryan Reilly, "Republicans Buy Into NRA's 'Fast and Furious' Gun Control Conspiracy Theory," *TPMMuckraker*, December 16, 2011; available online at: http://tpmmuckraker.talkingpointsmemo.com/2011/12/republicans_buy_into_nras_fast_and_furious_gun_control_conspiracy_theory.php.

27. Chris Brown, "2011: A Year in the NRA's 'Insane Paranoid' Conspiracy Theories," *Media Matters for America*, December 27, 2011; available online at: http://mediamatters.org/blog/201112220019.

28. MSNBC, *Hardball* with Chris Matthews, September 27, 2011.

29. Interview with anonymous source by Katie Pavlich.

30. Jorge Ramos, "Interview of President Barack Obama," Univision, March 23, 2011.

31. Ronald Kolb, "Fast and Furious in a Rotten Nutshell," *American Thinker*, October 7, 2011; available online at: http://www.americanthinker.com/2011/10/fast_and_furious_in_a_rotten_nutshell.html.

32. Jorge Ramos, "Interview of President Barack Obama," op. cit., 30.

33. Letter to ATF Acting Director Kenneth Melson from Oversight and Government Reform Committee Chairman Darrell Issa, March 16, 2011; available online at: www.cbsnews.com/htdocs/pdf/IssaLettertoATF_031611.pdf.

Chapter Seven

1. "Issa, Quigley Announce Bipartisan Transparency Caucus," House Oversight and Government Reform Committee press release, March 24, 2011; available online at: http://oversight.house.gov/index.php?option=com_content&task=view&id=629&Itemid=29.

2. Letter from Issa to Melson, March 16, 2011.

3. Chris Scholl, "Issa subpoenas ATF over gunwalking allegations," CBS News, April 1, 2011; available online at: http://www.cbsnews.com/8301-31727_162-20049764-10391695.html.

4. "Chairman Issa Subpoenas ATF for 'Project Gunrunner' Documents," House Oversight and Government Reform Committee press release April 1, 2011; available online at: http://oversight.house.gov/index.php?option=com_content&view=article&id=1231:chairman-issa-subpoenas-atf-for-project-gunrunner-documents-&catid=22:releasesstatements.

5. Letter from Assistant Attorney General Ronald Weich to Chairman Darrell Issa, April 8, 2011.

6. Letter from Darrell Issa to Justice Department, April 20, 2011.

7. You can watch the exchange between Issa and Holder at http://www.youtube.com/watch?v=4NqH88cSBqI.

8. "Operation Fast and Furious: Reckless Decisions, Tragic Outcomes," 112th Cong., June 15, 2011, statement of ATF Special Agent John Dodson.

9. Special Agent Peter Forcelli testimony, June 16, 2011; available online at: http://politicsarizona.com/2011/09/06/transcript-of-fast-furious-testimony-before-congress-implicating-dennis-burke/.

10. Ibid., statement of Josephine Terry, Brian Terry's mother.

11. Josephine Terry, statement in testimony before the House Oversight Committee, June 15, 2011.

12. Ibid.

13. "Operation Fast and Furious: Reckless Decisions, Tragic Outcomes," 112th Cong., June 15, 2011, statement of Ronald Weich, Assistant Attorney General.

14. ATF Briefing paper, "ATF Phoenix Field Division Phoenix Group VII (Gunrunner/Strike Force)," January 8, 2010.

15. "Operation Fast and Furious: Reckless Decisions, Tragic Outcomes," 112th Cong., June 15, 2011.

16. Lori Gliha, "Arizona US Attorney resigns and ATF acting director is reassigned," ABC News 15 Phoenix, August 30, 2011; available online at: http://www.abc15.com/dpp/news/local_news/investigations/az-us-attorney-resigns-and-atf-acting-director-is-reassigned-.

17. Moe Lane, "Fast and Furious Update: Kenneth Melson's Secret Testimony," *Red State*, July 6, 2011; available online at: http://www.redstate.com/moe_lane/2011/07/06/fast-and-furious-update-ken-melsons-secret-testimony/.

18. Kenneth Melson, "ATF Director: DOJ Response to Fast and Furious Investigation Intended to Protect Political Appointees," Committee on Oversight and Government Reform; available online at: http://oversight.house.gov/index.php?option=com_content&task=view&id=1383&Itemid=29.

19. Dennis Wagner, "Burke of Fast and Furious had anti-gun history," *The Arizona Republic*, January 28, 2012; available online at: http://www.azcentral.com/arizonarepublic/news/articles/2012/01/27/20120127dennis-burke-fast-furious-scandal-career.html.

20. Kim Murphy, "U.S. AK-47s linked to Mexican attorney's slaying," *Los Angeles Times*, June 23, 2011; available online at: http://articles.latimes.com/2011/jun/23/nation/la-na-gunrunner-20110623.

21. United States Congress, *The Department of Justice's Operation Fast and Furious: Fueling Cartel Violence*, July 26, 2011; available online at: http://oversight.house.gov/images/stories/Reports/FINAL_FINAL.pdf.

22. Ken Ellingwood, Richard Serrano, and Tracy Wilkinson, "Mexico Still Waiting for Answers on Fast and Furious Gun Program," *Los Angeles Times*, September 19, 2011.

23. "Mexico Asks U.S. to Extradite Alleged Gunrunners," *Latin American Tribune*, November 2011.

24. "Operation Fast and Furious: The Other Side of the Border," Oversight and Government Reform Committee, 112th Cong., July 26, 2011, statement of Darren Gil, former ATF Attaché to Mexico.

25. Victoria Nuland, "Deputy Secretary's Travel to Mexico August 15-17," U.S. Department of State, press statement, August 12, 2011; available online at: http://www.state.gov/r/pa/prs/ps/2011/08/170459.htm.

26. Interview with anonymous source by Katie Pavlich, December 11, 2011.

Chapter Eight

1. Transcript of interview with Special Agent Number 2, Office of Darrell Issa available online at: http://www.google.com/url?sa=t&rct=j&q=&esrc=s&source=web&cd=1&ved=0CCMQFjAA&url=http%3A%2F%2Fdailycaller.com%2Fwp-content%2Fuploads%2F2011%2F06%2Fissa-to-atf-dont-retaliate.pdf&ei=V5MyT6iBBaXY2QXRrvSfCQ&usg=AFQjCNGyLsdi4PvjoOJl7dtZyj0nvZ2iw.

2.   Interview with Jay Dobyns by Katie Pavlich, October 20, 2011.

3.   Interview with anonymous source by Katie Pavlich, December 11, 2011.

4.   Interview with anonymous source by Katie Pavlich December 11, 2011.

5.   Interview with anonymous source by Katie Pavlich December 11, 2011.

6.   Interview with anonymous source by Katie Pavlich December 11, 2011.

7.   Vince Cefalu, "Diary of an ATF Whistleblower," *Townhall Magazine*, February 2011.

8.   Cathy Scott, *The Rough Guide to True Crime* (Rough Guides, 2009).

9.   Vince Cefalu, "Diary of an ATF Whistleblower.".

10. Interview with Vince Cefalu by Katie Pavlich, November 12, 2011.

11. Vince Cefalu, "Diary of an ATF Whistleblower."

12. Ibid.

13. Interview with Peter Forcelli by Katie Pavlich, November 28, 2011.

14. "ATF Whistleblowers Question SW Border Strategy," Office of Senator Charles Grassley, press release; available online at: http://www.grassley.senate.gov/about/ATF-Whistleblowers-Question-SW-Border-Strategy.cfm#.

15. Congressman Darrell Issa, letter to ATF Deputy Director William Hoover, June 21, 2011, p. 2.

Chapter Nine

1.   "Operation Fast and Furious: The Other Side of the Border," before the Government Oversight and Reform Committee, 112th Cong., July 26, 2011, statement of Bill Newell, Special Agent in Charge ATF Phoenix Field Division; available online at: http://oversight.house.gov/index.php?option=com_content&view=article&id=1385%3A7-26-11-qoperation-fast-and-furious-the-other-side-of-the-borderq&catid=12&Itemid=20.

2.   Emails quoted in Matthew Boyle, "Despite new disclosures, White House maintains senior officials didn't know ATF was 'letting guns walk,'" *Daily Caller*, October 2, 2011; available online at: http://dailycaller.com/2011/10/02/despite-new-disclosures-white-house-maintains-senior-officials-didnt-know-atf-was-letting-guns-walk/.

3.   Email from William Newell to Kevin O'Reilly, September 3, 2010; available online at: http://www.scribd.com/doc/67142858/2/PHOENIX-GRIT-SEIZURES.

4.   Email from Kevin O'Reilly to William Newell, September 3 2010; available online at: http://www.scribd.com/doc/67142858/2/PHOENIX-GRIT-SEIZURES.

5. Darrell Issa, letter to Assistant to the President and National Security Advisor Thomas E. Donilon, September 9, 2011; available online at: www.cbsnews.com/ htdocs/pdf/whtey.pdf.

6. Jim Geraghty and Cam Edwards, "The Scandal of 'Gun-Walking,'" *National Review Online*, March 28, 2011; available online at: http://www.nationalreview. com/articles/263117/scandal-gunwalking-jim-geraghty.

7. Director Michael Walther to Attorney General Eric Holder, July 5, 2010, National Drug Intelligence Center, Weekly Report for July 5 Through July 9, 2010; available online at: http://www.cbsnews.com/8301-31727_162-20115038-10391695.html.

8. Assistant Attorney General Lanny Breuer to Attorney General Eric Holder, November 1, 2010, Re: Weekly Reports to Attorney General.

9. "Issa to Holder: You Own Fast and Furious," House Oversight Committee, press release, October 7, 2011; available online at: http://www.foxnews.com/interac tive/politics/2011/10/10/issa-responds-to-holder-letter-to-house-oversight-panel/.

10. Carrie Johnson, "Holder Takes Heat Over 'Fast and Furious' Scandal," NPR, October 6, 2011; available online at: http://www.npr.org/2011/10/06/141124685/ holder-takes-heat-over-fast-and-furious-scandal.

11. "Issa to Holder: You Own Fast and Furious," House Oversight Committee, press release, October 7, 2011.

12. Interview with Representative Paul Gosar by Katie Pavlich, September 2010.

13. Katie Pavlich, "White House: Holder Testimony 'Consistent and Truthful,'" *Townhall.com*, October 6, 2011; available online at: http://townhall.com/tipsheet/ katiepavlich/2011/10/06/white_house_holder_testimony_consistent_ and_truthful.

14. Carrie Johnson, "Holder Takes Heat Over 'Fast and Furious' Scandal," op. cit., 10.

15. "Federal Gun Smuggling Sting Operation, Part 2," before the House Judiciary Committee, 112th Cong., statement of Darrell Issa, Congressman, December 8, 2011; available online at: http://www.c-spanvideo.org/program/StingO.

16. Ibid.

17. Jonathan Strong, "Justice Department Reveals Origins of False Gun Letter to Grassley," *Roll Call*, December 2, 2011; available online at: http://www.rollcall. com/news/justice_department_reveals_origins_of_false_gun_letter_to_ grassley-210742-1.html.

18. "Grassley Calls for Resignation of Justice Department Official in Gunwalking Tragedy," Office of Senator Charles Grassley, press release, December 7, 2011; available online at: http://www.grassley.senate.gov/news/Article.cfm?customel_ dataPageID_1502=38173.

19. Interview with Peter Forcelli by Katie Pavlich, November 28, 2011.

20. Justice Department Oversight, Before the Senate Judiciary Committee, 112th Cong., November 8, 2011, statement by Eric Holder, Attorney General.

21. Ibid.

22. Eric Holder's Testimony to Sen. John Cornyn and the Senate Judiciary Committee, NRA News, November 8, 2011; video retrieved February 12, 2011, from http://www.youtube.com/watch?v=3S-LOiO_Q2U.

23. Matthew Boyle, "Now, 91 congressmen have 'no confidence' in Holder or believe he should quit," *The Daily Caller*. December 20, 2011; available online at: http://dailycaller.com/2011/12/20/now-90-congressmen-have-no-confidence-in-holder-or-believe-he-should-quit/.

24. Katie Pavlich, Twitter direct message to Matthew Boyle, January 29, 2012.

25. Monty Wilkinson, email message to Dennis Burke, December 15, 2011.

26. Terry Frieden, "Holder: 'Fast and Furious' Operation Didn't Reach DOJ 'Upper Levels,'" CNN *Justice*, September 7, 2011; available online at: http://articles.cnn.com/2011-09-07/us/holder.fast.and.furious_1_fast-and-furious-operation-atf-justice-department?_s=PM:US.

27. Justice Department Oversight, Before the Senate Judiciary Committee, 112th Cong, November 8, 2011, statement by Eric Holder, Attorney General.

28. Ibid.

29. Katie Pavlich, interview with anonymous source December 11, 2011.

Chapter Ten

1. Cam Edwards, "Chris Cox," NRANews Radio *Cam&Company*, November 17, 2010.

2. "Statement of Deputy Attorney General James Cole Regarding Information Requests for Multiple Sales of Semi-Automatic Rifles with Detachable Magazines," Department of Justice press release, July 11, 2011; available online at: http://www.justice.gov/opa/pr/2011/July/11-dag-900.html.

3. Interview with Arizona Representative Paul Gosar by Katie Pavlich, September 2011.

4. Interview with anonymous source, December 11, 2011.

5. Matthew Boyle, "New border gun rules a distraction from Fast and Furious scandal, Issa says," *Daily Caller*, July 11, 2011; available online: http://dailycaller.com/2011/07/11/new-border-gun-rules-a-distraction-from-fast-and-furious-scandal-issa-says/.

6. "New Reporting Requirements for Federal Firearms Licensees on the Southwest Border," Office of Senator Charles Grassley press release, July 11, 2011; available

online at: http://www.grassley.senate.gov/news/Article.cfm?customel_dataPageID_1502=35929.

7. "Fierce Battle Over Gun Rights," Fox News, August 5, 2011; video available online at: http://video.foxnews.com/v/1095760427001/fierce-battle-over-gun-rights/.

8. "Attorney General Eric Holder Announces Results of International Child Pornography Investigation at Operation Delego Press Conference," Department of Justice, August 3, 2011; available online at: http://www.justice.gov/iso/opa/ag/speeches/2011/ag-speech-110803.html.

9. Lynn Sweet, "Obama, Calderon Mexico City Press Conference Transcript," *Sun-Times*, April 17, 2009; available online at: http://blogs.suntimes.com/sweet/2009/04/obama_calderon_mexico_city_pre.html

10. President Ronald Reagan, "Address to the Nation on the Iran Arms and Contra Aid Controversy," Washington, D.C., March 4, 1987; available online at: University of Texas, http://www.reagan.utexas.edu/archives/speeches/1987/030487h.htm.

11. Matthew Boyle, "Issa says Holder should apologize to Mexico: 'Justice has blood on their hands" Daily Caller, January 26, 2012; available online at: http://dailycaller.com/2012/01/26/issa-says-holder-should-apologize-to-mexico-justice-has-blood-on-their-hands/.

12. Comment made by Rahm Emanuel in the Wall Street Journal CEO Council, "Shaping the New Agenda," 2008.

13. Sean Hannity, "Holder in the Hot Seat," Fox News Channel, December 8, 2011.

14. "Operation Fast and Furious: Reckless Decisions, Tragic Outcomes," 112th Cong., June 15, 2011, statement of ATF Special Agent John Dodson.

15. Richard Serrano, "White House received emails about Fast and Furious gun-trafficking operation," *Los Angeles Times*, September 2, 2011; available online at: http://articles.latimes.com/2011/sep/02/nation/la-na-atf-guns-20110902.

16. Chris Cox, "Holder tells Congress the Obama administration wants to ban guns," *Daily Caller*, February 8, 2012; available online at: http://dailycaller.com/2012/02/08/holder-tells-congress-the-obama-administration-wants-to-ban-guns/.

17. "Oversight of the U.S. Department of Justice," before the Senate Judiciary Committee, 112th Cong., November 8, 2011, statement of Darrell Issa, Congressman.

18. Lydia Saad, "Self-Reported Gun Ownership in U.S. Is Highest Since 1993," *Gallup Politics*, October 26, 2011; available online at: http://www.gallup.com/poll/150353/Self-Reported-Gun-Ownership-Highest-1993.aspx.

19. Jeffrey M. Jones, "Record-Low 26% in U.S Favor Handgun Ban," *Gallup Politics*, October 26, 2011; available online at: http://www.gallup.com/poll/150341/record-low-favor-handgun-ban.aspx.

20. James Oliphant, "She's a White House veteran," *Los Angeles Times*, May 11, 2010; available online at: http://articles.latimes.com/2010/may/11/nation/la-na-kagan-profile-20100511.

21. Brian Darling, "Fact: Kagan in Anti-Second Amendment," *Redstate*, July 1, 2010; available online at: http://www.redstate.com/brian_d/2010/07/01/fact-kagan-is-anti-second-amendment/.

22. *McDonald v. City of Chicago*, Illinois, 561 U.S. (2010).

23. Adam Lipik, "Justices Extend Firearms Rights in 5-to-4 Ruling," *New York Times*, June 28, 2010; available online at: http://www.nytimes.com/2010/06/29/us/29scotus.html.

24. James Oliphant, "GOP blocks Obama's pick for D.C. appeals court," *Los Angeles Times*, December 6, 2011; available online at: http://articles.latimes.com/2011/dec/06/news/la-pn-gop-blocks-appeals-court-20111206.

25. Wayne LaPierre, "The Obama Administration is Planning a Second-Term Attack on Gun Rights," *Daily Caller*, December 12, 2011; available online at: http://home.nra.org/iphone.aspx/blog/290.

26. Statement of Secretary Hillary Clinton, "U.S. Support for the Arms Trade Treaty," U.S. Department of State press release, October 14, 2009; available online at: http://www.state.gov/secretary/rm/2009a/10/130573.htm.

27. Rachel Stohl, "U.S. Policy and the Arms Trade Treaty," working paper commissioned by Project Ploughshares as a briefing for the round-table event, "Towards a Global Arms Trade Treaty (ATT): What role for the United States?" held in Washington, D.C., February 2010.

28. Ted R. Bromund, Ph.D., "Why the U.S. Should Be Concerned About the Domestic Effects of the U.N. Arms Trade Treaty," the Heritage Foundation, December 13, 2011; available online at: http://www.heritage.org/research/reports/2011/12/effects-of-the-un-arms-trade-treaty-on-the-us.

29. Ibid.

30. Emily Miller, "Obama's fast and furious spin," Washington Times, Feburary 15, 2012; available online at: http://m.washingtontimes.com/news/2012/feb/15/obamas-fast-and-furious-spin/.

31. William La Jeunesse, "U.S. Attorney's Office Rejects Family of Murdered Border Patrol Agent as Crime Victims," Fox News, August 11, 2011; available online at: http://www.foxnews.com/politics/2011/08/11/us-attorneys-office-rejects-family-slain-border-patrol-agent-as-crime-victims/.

32. Chairman Darrell Issa on CBS *Face the Nation*, October 16, 2011; transcript available online at: http://www.cbsnews.com/stories/2011/10/16/ftn/main20121072.shtml.

33. Email to redacted from redacted, December 15, 2010.

34. Email to redacted from George Gillett, December 15, 2010.

35. Mike Levine, "Justice Department Accuses Issa of 'Mischaracterizing' Evidence in Probe of Operation Fast and Furious," Fox News, October 17, 2011; available online at: http://www.foxnews.com/politics/2011/10/17/justice-department-accuses-issa-mischaracterizing-evidence-in-probe-operation/?test=latestnews.

INDEX